40 Pubs  170 Beers

Real Ale

RECORD BOOK

ADRIAN TIERNEY-JONES

First published 2010

The History Press
The Mill, Brimscombe Port
Stroud, Gloucestershire, GL5 2QG
www.thehistorypress.co.uk

British Library Cataloguing in Publication Data.
A catalogue record for this book is available from the British Library.

ISBN 978 0 7524 5715 4

Typesetting and origination by The History Press
Printed in Great Britain

Cover: © CBW/Alamy
All other images from iStockphoto
except p.17, courtesy of Dark Star
Brewery; p.21, courtesy of London
Pride Brewery; p.25, courtesy of
Shepherd Neame Brewery; p.31,
courtesy of The Queen's Arms, Corton
Denham; p.35, courtesy of Exmoor
Brewery; p.39, courtesy of Skinner's
Brewery; p.45, courtesy of The Walter
de Cantelupe, Kempsey; p.49, courtesy
of The Grainstore Brewery; p.63,
courtesy of Greene King; p.67, courtesy
of Wells Brewery; p.72, courtesy of The
Creek Inn, Isle of Man; p.76, courtesy
of Hawkshead Brewery; p.87, courtesy
of The Fleece Inn, Haworth; p.91,
courtesy of Sharp's Brewery; p.95,
courtesy of Saltaire Brewery; p.117,
courtesy of Brew Dog; p.123, courtesy
of Hilden Brewery.

CONTENTS

INTRODUCTION

Back in the 1980s and 1990s admit to liking a drop of cask beer and you would have been typecast as a tubby, Arran sweater-wearing, well-bearded chap with a fondness for hanging pewter tankards on your belt. Lager was the drink that the smart folk drank. The branding was hip and modern, and lager was seen as reassuringly expensive. Cask ale on the other hand was what your grandfather drank.

There was also the small matter of temperature and quality. After the initial success of cask ale, too many pubs thought it necessary to install banks of handpumps, sometimes offering up to a dozen ales. What many of them didn't realise was that cask beer is a living product and needs to be drunk within three days (sometimes their cellar didn't have the right temperature for ale either). The unwitting drinker, willing to give cask a chance, was often put off when served a pint of well-vinegared ale that had been sitting around for several days – and back to lager they went. In the mid-1990s, cask beer was also hammered by the emergence of nitro-keg beers such as Caffrey's.

In the past decade, the situation has changed beyond all recognition. Cask beer, real ale, whatever you want to call it, is growing in popularity. No longer is it saddled with its old image; if anything it's the premium lagers that look a little fuddy-duddy while ale (possibly helped by Madonna's endorsement of Timothy Taylor's Landlord on the *Jonathan Ross Show* in 2003) has a more go-ahead, aspirational image. The likes of Greene King, SA Brains and Fuller's are involved in sponsoring major sporting events and teams, while the interest in local food, organic produce and free-range lifestyles has also painted cask beer in a positive light.

The need to present the beer in the very best quality and at the right temperature was boosted by the success of Cask Marque, an organisation that helps pubs serve their beers in the optimum state. The number of breweries has grown over the past few years and in 2010 stands at over 700. Some are small one-man operations, while others are more ambitious and see their beers travel all over the UK. And let us not forget the family regional breweries who have redoubled their efforts to sell beer and also innovate — the usual bitter and golden ale are joined in many instances by an IPA, a mild, porter and beers made with honey or flavoured with various fruits.

Even though up to 40 pubs are said to be closing weekly, those that major in cask beer tend to be thriving and successful as people seek them out, compare notes on the beers they stock and badger the landlord for information on future brews. CAMRA's regular beer festivals also spread the word. And here is where this book becomes an essential bit of travel kit. Here you will find nearly 200 beers from breweries up and down the country, beers demonstrating that cask ale has a multitude of flavours and aromas, styles and moods. If you want a chocolate stout then look no further, while those with a penchant for a highly hopped IPA will find the very same within. There are also recommended pubs, information on how to taste beer and a reading list. Beer is our national drink and this book will help you celebrate it. Cheers!

THE WORLD OF BEER STYLES

BITTER

Beer was described as 'bitter' in the mid-nineteenth century, but this was probably just a reference to the effect produced by a high hopping rate rather than the identification of a new style. It wasn't until the end of the Victorian age that bitter emerged in its own right, mainly as a result of the big family brewers producing beers that didn't need to mature for as long as porter or IPA; these 'running beers' could then be sold through their pubs. The best English bitters strike a balance between crisp, biscuity maltiness and a citrus and fruity hop character, with the bite of bitterness in the mix. They can be any colour from pale straw to deep russet. In strength they are usually around 3.5–3.8% for an ordinary bitter and 4–4.5% for a best bitter, whilst special or premium is stronger still. Golden ales are not bitters in the old sense of the word but often fall into the same style camp.

INDIA PALE ALE

A nineteenth-century beer sent out to India and enjoyed back in the UK. They were highly hopped and strong in alcohol. In the twentieth century IPA rather lost its way, but the last 20 years has seen it revived, helped in part by American craft brewers' variation on the style.

PORTER

Strong and dark ale of the eighteenth century, though it declined in the nineteenth century as the fashion for golden IPAs took hold and the emerging middle classes wanted to distance themselves from a drink mainly imbibed by the workers. Brewing porter also became uneconomic as it was stored for months in big vats, while lighter, weaker beers could be sent out to pubs and drunk within a matter of weeks. Porter had virtually vanished by the 1980s until British and American microbrewers started making it again.

STOUT

Strong porters were called 'stout' porters (porter and stout are the same many would argue) while Guinness produced the distinctive Irish Dry Stout with its roast bite. English stouts have a less assertive roastiness and a mite more fruitiness (plums, currants). Imperial Russian stouts and porters, milk stout, oatmeal stout and sweet stout are variations on a dark theme.

MILD

Originally received its name became it was young and fresh, compared to vatted porters. Wrongly thought to mean a beer low in hops, even though that is the case now. Most milds are low in alcohol and dark, though there are also light milds and strong ones.

SPECIALITY BEERS

Brewers add all sorts of things to their beer, from fruit and veg to spices, chocolate, coffee beans and vanilla pods. Beers are also aged in wooden barrels, some from the whisky trade, others from rum and even wine. Some brewers are trying their hand at lagered beers, a source of contention. Some would say a cask-conditioned lager is an oxymoron (though some would point to kellerbier or even Zoigl), while others would say as long as it tastes good who cares?

CASK CONDITIONED

Prior to the onset of kegged beers in the years following the end of the Second World War, the majority of beers served by handpump in the pub would have been cask conditioned. In the 1970s the term 'real ale' was coined for these beers by the Campaign For Real Ale and its members took up arms against what they saw as a tide of dead and fizzy beers supplanting their traditional heroes (Watney's Red Barrel was a particular target for their ire).

For a beer to be 'real', it needs to undergo a secondary fermentation in the cask as it sits in the pub cellar, thanks to the presence of yeast working away, maturing the beer and producing a fuller flavour as well as natural carbonation. Once the cask is broached the beer within needs to be drunk as quickly as possibly, usually within three days, otherwise it is spoilt – taste a beer when it has just been tapped and try the same cask three days later and there will be a definite difference in the mouthfeel and flavour.

Before beer can be served, casks are tapped and vented, a process of drawing off some of the carbon dioxide that has been produced by the secondary fermentation. Temperature is also important at this stage. Pub cellars should be kept at about 11°C (52°F), though some brewers serve their beers slightly cooler, especially in pubs where there is a young clientele used to the mouth-numbingly cold temperatures of some lagers. Beer from which yeast has been filtered is called brewery conditioned – it will not improve or mature.

HOW TO TASTE BEER

Look at it. It should be clear (unless it's a wheat beer).

Check its condition. A well-conditioned beer should dance, not flop, on the tongue.

Swirl the beer in the glass to release its aromas.

Note the beer's colour.

One of the great joys of a beer is its aroma. Amongst other things, malty aromas can suggest dried fruit, coffee beans, biscuit, smoke, malt, Ovaltine, plain chocolate, toffee, butterscotch and caramel. Hoppy aromas can be either fruity, resiny, aromatic, citrusy, peppery, herbal, spicy, lemony or floral. It's possible to pick out Seville orange marmalade (sometimes even lime), tropical fruits such as lychees and passion fruit, resin (think varnish), blackcurrants and even fruit-flavoured candy. With some of the stronger beers the yeast esters add their own complexities such as tropical fruit, banana, apricot skin and a spritzy feel.

Tasting the beer. Some beers come bearing plenty of fruity flavours, while others boast rich, malty savours. What is the essence of the beer in your mouth? Is it smooth, tingling, grainy, thin, acidic or chewy? Some beers are robust on the palate while others slip down like honey.

Do swallow. Unlike wine-tasting, part of beer-tasting involves letting the beer work its effect on your throat. In classic English bitters you will feel the dryness and bitterness.

Consider the beer's finish. Is it bitter? Is it dry? Does it last? Does a hint of malt return? Does it make you want another? It should.

SOUTH-EAST ENGLAND

Even though the Cockney hop-pickers are long gone and many oast-houses are now bijou dwellings, the hop fields of Kent still exert an influence on the region as the hoppy beers of Shepherd Neame demonstrate. Next door in Sussex, Harvey's flies the flag for distinctive beers. Their masterful Sussex Best Bitter positively jumps out of the glass with its muscular hop nose; try their bottle-conditioned Imperial Russian Stout, one of the world's greatest beers. London's role as a brewing centre has long been lost, with Fuller's the only surviving traditional family brewery. However, the makers of London Pride continue to excel with a wonderful variety of beers and the capital is also home to Meantime, whose brewmaster Alastair Hook trained in Bavaria. Elsewhere in the region, the beer scene thrives: Brakspear Bitter remains a classic pint and Hook Norton pump out a goodly selection of ales, as do the likes of Loddon, Ascot and Vale.

Turf Tavern, Bath Place, Oxford

Famous and historic pub hidden away down an alley, built right next to the old city walls. Low ceilings, several rooms and nearly a dozen real ales on display; meanwhile the courtyard in the shadow of the wall is made for sunny afternoons to be spent considering and contemplating a glass of beer.

Date:

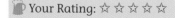 Your Rating: ☆ ☆ ☆ ☆ ☆

Royal Oak, Tabard Street, Borough, London

Down Tabard Street, supposedly close to the long-gone inn from where Chaucer's merry pilgrims departed for Canterbury, is where you will find this unpretentious corner street, two-room pub. As this is the sole London house of Lewes brewers Harvey's, pilgrims in search of their ales come to pay their respects.

Date:

Your Rating: ☆ ☆ ☆ ☆ ☆

Black Boy, Wharf Hill, Winchester

Multi-roomed town pub that is jammed to the gunnels with all manner of curios, such as stuffed animals (including a baboon in a kilt), several rows of old fire buckets and shelf after shelf of old books. Friendly and comfortable atmosphere that is helped by a judicious quintet of locally brewed cask beers.

Date:

Your Rating: ☆ ☆ ☆ ☆ ☆

Evening Star, Surrey Street, Brighton

Former home of Dark Star who began brewing there in 1994 before moving out to bigger premises (though they still own the pub). The décor is scrubbed wooden floors and rustic and robust wooden furniture, a worthy environment in which to celebrate Dark Star's wonderful beers, including Hophead and Espresso.

Date:

🍺 Your Rating: ☆ ☆ ☆ ☆ ☆

The Coastguard, St Margaret's Bay, Dover

The Coastguard has its back to the White Cliffs of Dover and faces the English Channel as it crashes on the shingle yards away. On a gorgeous day view cross-Channel ferries from the outside terrace, but once winter kicks in retreat to the compact bar. Four real ales and a handsome selection of foreign bottled beers are available.

Date:

🍺 Your Rating: ☆ ☆ ☆ ☆ ☆

Ascot Ales Anastasia's Imperial Stout, 8%

Supercharged version of the brewery's Anastasia's Exile Stout, which is a more manageable 5%. As dark as the deepest ocean, the nose offers roasted coffee beans, chocolate and the warmth of alcohol; the palate is a rich, chewy, sensual experience, with dark fruits, coffee and liquorice before its deep spirited finish.

Date:

Your Rating: ☆ ☆ ☆ ☆ ☆

Bowman Ales Swift One, 3.8%

This Hampshire brewery started operations in 2006 and Swift One has been a major award winner. It's not hard to see why as this gorgeous blonde-coloured beer has oodles of fruit on the nose, a trait that continues through the palate before a dry finish that tips its hat towards a pleasing hint of sweetness.

Date:

Your Rating: ☆ ☆ ☆ ☆ ☆

Brakspear Bitter 3.4%

Famous Thames Valley ale brewed in Henley before moving to Witney from where it remains fabulous. Light ruby/amber in colour; the nose pulsates with rich malt and spicy peppery hop aromas while the palate is grainy and biscuity before a citric orange peel fruitiness makes its entrance; there is bitterness and dryness in the finish.

Date:

Your Rating: ☆ ☆ ☆ ☆ ☆

Dark Star
Espresso, 4.2%

Real coffee is used in the making of this edgy dark beer, which probably shouldn't be drunk too late at night. Topped with a collar of foam straight out of Starbucks, the nose is roast coffee beans (Italian), while the palate is rich and roasted with lots more coffee (veering towards mocha) before its dry, bitter finish.

Date:

Your Rating: ☆ ☆ ☆ ☆ ☆

Dark Star
Hophead, 3.8%

Hops have always been central to the beers of this Brighton-based brewery and its bestseller Hophead is no exception to the rule. Even though it's a mere 3.8%, this is a beer whose nose is a fragrant delight of flowery and elderflower notes, while the palate has more tropical fruit and a long dry finish.

Date:

Your Rating: ☆ ☆ ☆ ☆ ☆

Fuller's
ESB, 5.5%

Classic strong ale from Fuller's which first saw the light of day in 1969. A multiple award-winner, it is dark amber in colour and has a pungent, sensual flurry of rich citrusy notes on the nose. The palate is balanced between a crisp graininess and orange cointreau-like notes before it concludes in a dry and long bitter finish.

Date:

Your Rating: ☆ ☆ ☆ ☆ ☆

Fuller's
London Pride, 4.1%

First launched on St George's Day in 1960, this is the lynchpin and bestseller of London's largest brewery. Ringing citrusy hop notes on the nose gallop on to a palate that executes an exquisite balance between more citrusy orange and fresh, crisp cracker-like notes with a hint of toffee. The finish is bittersweet.

Date:

🍺 Your Rating: ☆ ☆ ☆ ☆ ☆

Harvey's
Porter, 4.8%

Based on a beer first brewed in 1859. The nose is a confection of dark fruit (plums, sultanas) and treacle toffee, along with whispers of liquorice on the nose. The palate sees treacle toffee, chocolate and vinous fruit notes, with hints of soot and smoke making a brief appearance. The lingering finish is dry and chewy.

Date:

🍺 Your Rating: ☆ ☆ ☆ ☆ ☆

Harvey's
Sussex Best Bitter, 4%

One of the classic bitters of England. On the nose there is a muscular and musky hop presence, while the palate is full-bodied without being too intrusive on the tastebuds, showing effortless balance between rich maltiness and more hoppiness. A slight sweetness in the background keeps any tendency to over-bitterness in check.

Date:

🍺 Your Rating: ☆ ☆ ☆ ☆ ☆

FULLER'S LONDON PRIDE

LONDON PRIDE

WHATEVER YOU DO, TAKE PRIDE.

Hogs Back
A Over T, 9%

Indulgent barley wine released every winter by this award-winning Surrey brewery – one for the fireside perhaps? Chestnut brown in colour, there's a powerful gust of dark fruit, accompanied by wafts of caramel sweetness and warming alcohol on the nose. The palate is fiery, rich, powerful and fruity, followed by a bittersweet, dry and alcoholic finish.

Date:

🍺 Your Rating: ☆ ☆ ☆ ☆ ☆

Hook Norton
Double Stout, 4.8%

One glimpse of the Victorian tower brewery of Hook Norton down an Oxfordshire country lane and the heart skips a beat. This glorious stout is pretty tremendous, too: as dark as the night just before the new moon, with a sensuous, luscious, creamy body and hints of chocolate-coated coffee beans.

Date:

🍺 Your Rating: ☆ ☆ ☆ ☆ ☆

Hook Norton
Old Hooky, 4.6%

The brewery's flagship ale, Old Hooky, is a firmly traditional country bitter with a confident (but never swaggering) character. Chestnut brown in colour, on the palate it possesses a silky maltiness plus hints of mocha coffee, which are bossed about by a rich and bold citrus fruitiness and ending with a crisp cracker-like dryness.

Date:

🍺 Your Rating: ☆ ☆ ☆ ☆ ☆

Hopdaemon
Incubus, 4%

Bestselling beer from a Kentish brewery that was set up in Newnham at the start of the new century. Bronze coloured, it has a floral hop nose and in the glass it is slightly sweet, toffeeish and harbours a hint of roast and chocolate notes. Hops used in the beer are grown two miles away.

Loddon
Ferryman's Gold, 4.4%

Oxfordshire-based brewery that first started dispensing beer in 2003. Ferryman's Gold was one of its first beers and has won many awards. Golden in the glass it has a sprightly aromatic and fruity nose suggestive of lychees, while the palate is smooth with more tropical fruit in the mix before its bittersweet finish.

Meantime
London Pale Ale, 4.7%

This is a classic example of a famous British beer style, albeit with an American twist (US hops are used to give a fresh and funky bouquet of fruit notes on the nose). In the mouth the high hop rate produces plenty of rich fruity notes, before it follows onto a dry and appetising finish.

Date:

Your Rating: ☆ ☆ ☆ ☆ ☆

Date:

Your Rating: ☆ ☆ ☆ ☆ ☆

Date:

Your Rating: ☆ ☆ ☆ ☆ ☆

Ramsgate Gadds Faithful Dogbolter, 5.6%

Dogbolter was an infamous strong ale brewed by the Firkin pub chain. Ramsgate Brewery's founder Eddie Gadds was a great fan of it (he also brewed for Firkin) and this is his loving tribute. A dark porter, it has mocha coffee and dustings of chocolate on the nose, while the palate is smooth, creamy and roasty leading to a dry and powerful finish.

Date:

Your Rating: ☆ ☆ ☆ ☆ ☆

Sambrook's Wandle, 3.8%

With the demise of Young's in 2006, brewing came to an end in the borough of Wandsworth, but a couple of years later Duncan Sambrook, a man with a mission and a mash tun, set up his eponymous brewery. Sambrook's debut beer is a pale-coloured session ale with a bittersweet character and a fruity, bitter finish.

Date:

Your Rating: ☆ ☆ ☆ ☆ ☆

Shepherd Neame Bishop's Finger, 5.2%

Reddish-brown strong bitter from one of England's oldest breweries, based in Faversham, Kent. Citrusy nose with hints of biscuit-like graininess in the background. The palate takes a brief bow in the direction of this biscuity maltiness (along with certain nuttiness and citrus fruit) before its long, bitter, mouth-tingling finish.

Date:

Your Rating: ☆ ☆ ☆ ☆ ☆

SHEPHERD NEAME

SINCE 1698

BISHOPS
FINGER

Surrey Hills
Ranmore Ale, 3.8%

Surrey Hills started brewing in 2005 in the picturesque Surrey village of Shere, though at the time of writing they are currently planning to relocate to near Dorking. This is one of their bestsellers, a straw-coloured bittersweet session beer with an appetising bitter finish that sets the drinker up for another sip.

Date:

Your Rating: ☆ ☆ ☆ ☆ ☆

Vale
Gravitas, 4.8%

Enticingly pale gold in colour, this is a beer that packs a perfumed punch on the nose of sweet pear drops and hints of honey. Poured into the glass and then tasted, it delights with a ravishingly light tropical fruit character that is balanced and beefed up by a satisfyingly dry and grainy finish.

Date:

Your Rating: ☆ ☆ ☆ ☆ ☆

Westerham
British Bulldog, 4.3%

Winston Churchill lived near Westerham and you could argue that this punchy best bitter is a worthy tribute to the great man. The nose offers a blend of earthy hoppy notes with a sprightly citrusy background, while the palate has more tart citrus, plus a grainy cereal crunchiness in the background before its last and final bitter finish.

Date:

Your Rating: ☆ ☆ ☆ ☆ ☆

TOP 10 BEERS

🍺 BEER

🍺 TASTING NOTES

BEER	TASTING NOTES
Ascot Ales Anastasia's Imperial Stout	
Bowman Ales Swift One	
Brakspear Bitter	
Fuller's ESB	
Harvey's Porter	
Harvey's Sussex Best Bitter	
Hook Norton Double Stout	
Hook Norton Old Hooky	
Meantime London Pale Ale	
Vale Gravitas	

SOUTH-WEST ENGLAND

One of the most curious beers of this region was the Victorian-era White Ale of South Devon; these rich and glutinous brews had their fans, even though they contained pigeon droppings. Nowadays, the South-West's cask ales are pigeon-free – from Cornwall to Gloucester and all points in between the region positively buzzes with a variety of beers. Forget cider (though it obviously has its place), the area is a powerhouse of brewing featuring dozens of micro-brewers and a clutch of well-established family breweries. Some of the beers, such as St Austell's Tribute or Skinner's Cornish Knocker, are delicately fruity with a hint of sweetness in the finish, while others (think Otter Head and Exmoor Beast) are the colour of an ancient mahogany sideboard and offer rich and robust sustenance. Brewing exploration is represented by the rural brews of Moor Beer, whose JJJ is a hop scorcher of a triple IPA.

The Bridge Inn, Bridge Hill, Topsham, Devon

Unique time machine of a pub – no piped music and no chips but plenty of locally brewed cask beers (six served straight from the barrel) and hearty and hardy sandwiches and pasties. There's no bar as such, but grab a seat in one of the two rooms and you'll be rooted there until closing time.

Date:

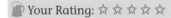 Your Rating: ☆ ☆ ☆ ☆ ☆

The Blue Anchor, Coinage -hall St, Helston, Cornwall

Venerable brewpub that started life in the fifteenth century as a rest house run by monks. It swiftly became a tavern and has stayed that way ever since. Inside, flagstone floor corridors separate several cosy rooms, in which a selection of 'Spingo' beers brewed out the back (including the 6.5% Special) can be enjoyed.

Date:

Your Rating: ☆ ☆ ☆ ☆ ☆

The Burbage, Prestbury, Cheltenham, Glos

It's a short gallop to Cheltenham racecourse from the Royal Oak and this nineteenth-century honey-coloured Cotswold stone pub hums with activity on race days. Beer-lovers will also jockey for position at the bar as the pub has also rightly gained a superb reputation for its selection of ales, many of which are brewed locally.

Date:

Your Rating: ☆ ☆ ☆ ☆ ☆

The Queens Arms, Corton Denham, Somerset

Stylish yet effortlessly comfortable pub that has the feel of Chelsea meets the countryside. The décor is calm, classic and collected: flagstones and wooden boards, cream-coloured walls and marble fireplace. West Country cask ales dominate the bar along with a guest from further afield, while there is an impressive selection of foreign bottled beer.

Date:

Your Rating: ☆ ☆ ☆ ☆ ☆

Woods, Bank Square, Dulverton, Somerset

Exmoor gem and a former bakery with an interior featuring loads of wood, exposed stone walls and a bar seemingly hewn out of an oak. The bar and dining room nestle cheek by jowl in a companionable way, and diners and drinkers mix and mingle in the very best traditions of pub democracy. West Country cask ales include St Austell's Proper Job.

Date:

Your Rating: ☆ ☆ ☆ ☆ ☆

Badger
First Gold, 4%

Renowned family brewers based in the town of Blandford Forum. Dark gold in colour, this has chocolate, toffee and faint roast notes on the nose with a hint of marmalade in the background. The mouthfeel is full-bodied with a delicate wispy chocolate and caramel character, balanced by a much richer and grown-up orange character. Dry finish.

Date:

Your Rating: ☆ ☆ ☆ ☆ ☆

Bath Ales
Dark Hare, 4%

Based in Bristol despite its name, Bath Ales produces a tremendous range of beers, but Dark Hare is its first foray into stout. With a nose producing lots of roasty notes, it's no surprise that the palate has a similar BBQ character, though also expect a creamy mouthfeel with coffee and chocolate making their presence felt. The finish is dry.

Date:

Your Rating: ☆ ☆ ☆ ☆ ☆

Box Steam
Funnel Blower, 4.5%

Wiltshire-based brewery that look to the work of Isambard Kingdom Brunel for their beer name inspiration. This dark chestnut brown porter is named after an explosion that took out a funnel on the SS *Great Eastern*. In the glass, roast notes vie for the drinker's attention with a gentle vanilla sweetness, making for a less explosive but still striking experience.

Date:

Your Rating: ☆ ☆ ☆ ☆ ☆

Bristol Beer Factory Milk Stout, 4.5%

Rare outing for a beer style that many thought had vanished with the British Empire or was solely confined to the hard-to-find Mackeson. Brewed in Bristol and holder of several best-of-show awards, it's a creamy and nourishing stout with roasted notes linking arms with a delicate sweetness to provide a wonderfully balanced beer.

Date:

Your Rating: ☆ ☆ ☆ ☆ ☆

Cotleigh Peregrine Porter, 5%

Down the hill from Exmoor Ales in Wiveliscombe, Cotleigh produces a full flight of beers whose names reflect the birdlife of nearby Exmoor. Peregrine is dark mahogany brown in colour. The nose has plenty of dark malt with fruit in the background, while the palate has more dark malt, chocolate and a fruity hoppiness. The finish is dry and grainy.

Date:

Your Rating: ☆ ☆ ☆ ☆ ☆

Country Life, Devonshire 10-Tender, 10%

Strong barley wine from the Big Sheep attraction in North Devon. Mainly in bottle, but rare casks are worth hunting out. Chestnut in colour, with a sweet, fruitcake nose. In the mouth full-bodied; tasting brings forth dark fruits, all wrapped up with a fiery alcoholic character and soothed by a malty smoothness. The finish mixes alcoholic warmth and hop tingle.

Date:

Your Rating: ☆ ☆ ☆ ☆ ☆

Dartmoor
Jail Ale, 4.8%

Dartmoor best bitter brewed a mile from the bleak edifice of one of England's most isolated prisons. Tan-brown in colour, the nose thrums with citrus fruit plus a hint of ripe peach skin. Subtly does it on the palate with a soft, caramel, toffee maltiness opening up the proceedings before the onset of a gorgeous thirst-quenching fruitiness; bittersweet finish.

Date:

Your Rating: ☆ ☆ ☆ ☆ ☆

Exmoor
Beast, 6.6%

Beast by name, beast by nature, this is a strong, dark porter whose lair is the Somerset town of Wiveliscombe. On the nose roasted espresso beans, sticky currants and raisins in a jar, cocoa and a fiery hint of brandy or rum. More fruitcake, alcohol, coffee beans, chocolate on the palate, all kept in line with a spicy hoppiness, before the complex long aftertaste.

Date:

Your Rating: ☆ ☆ ☆ ☆ ☆

Hop Back
Summer Lightning, 5%

Golden ale, which, although not the first (that was Exmoor Gold), was the one that inspired others. Nose is ripe peach skin, newly mown grass, white pepper and faint wisps of lychee. First impressions on the palate are the bitterness, not frightening but friendly. On the palate fruit (banana, nectarine?), a good mid-palate of grainy malt with a long bitter and dry finish.

Date:

Your Rating: ☆ ☆ ☆ ☆ ☆

EXMOOR

BEAST

STRONG ALE

500ml ℮

Alc. 6.6% Vol.

Keystone
Dark Porter, 5.5%

Wiltshire brewery set up by former army officer Alasdair Large. Dark chestnut in colour, the nose has milk chocolate, cocoa powder, milky coffee and a hint of blackcurrant, while the palate suggests mocha coffee and chocolate, and has a creamy and silky character that leads to a crunchy, crisp dryness, a soothing creaminess and a counterpoint of bitterness.

Date:

Your Rating: ☆ ☆ ☆ ☆ ☆

Moor
JJJ, 9%

Moor is run by enthusiastic Californian Justin Hawke, who is naturally influenced by the can-do attitude of the craft breweries of his homeland. He loves hops as well, a passion that is all too evident in this Triple IPA, an indecently hoppy and pungent bruiser of a beer, with a glorious fruitiness keeping the hop from being overwhelming.

Date:

Your Rating: ☆ ☆ ☆ ☆ ☆

O'Hanlons
Port Stout, 4.8%

Brewery founder John O'Hanlon recalled a hangover cure of a glass of stout with port added; that was the basis of this luscious and luxurious beer. Dark chestnut in colour, its nose has mocha coffee, milk chocolate and a hint of roasted barley. The palate is coffee, chocolate and roasted malt with the sweetness of the port in the background. The finish is dry and grainy.

Date:

Your Rating: ☆ ☆ ☆ ☆ ☆

Otter
Head, 5.8%

Strong beer from this eco-conscious brewery based outside Honiton. Chestnut brown in colour, it has vinous notes and roasted malt vying for attention on the nose. On the palate, there are nutty, vinous, biscuity, rye-cracker dryness notes with a background of chocolate orange. The finish is dry and malty.

Date:

Your Rating: ☆ ☆ ☆ ☆ ☆

RCH
East Street Cream, 5%

A former cider-works near Weston-super-Mare is home to RCH, though the brewery began at the Royal Clarence Hotel (hence the name) in Highbridge. First brewed in 1995, East Street Cream is chestnut brown in colour with fruit-cake notes and a hint of Muscat grape on the nose. The fruity theme continues on the palate leading to a dry and grainy finish.

Date:

Your Rating: ☆ ☆ ☆ ☆ ☆

St Austell
Proper Job, 4.5%

Cornish family brewery whose head brewer Roger Ryman has attracted awards and plaudits since joining in the late 1990s. This fruity IPA style is the result of a sabbatical at Bridgport Brewery in the US, offering a scintillating nose of tropical fruit (lychees) and citrus, before its zesty, fruity effect on the palate and a dry refreshing finish.

Date:

Your Rating: ☆ ☆ ☆ ☆ ☆

Severn Vale
Severn Sins, 5.2%

Micro-brewery based on a farm outside the Gloucestershire town of Dursley. This is an award-winning stout, as dark as the deepest depths of the ocean, and just as perilous if over-indulged in. Roast coffee beans and currants on the nose are followed by a rich and smoky palate while the finish is dry and bitter.

Date:

Your Rating: ☆ ☆ ☆ ☆ ☆

Sharp's
Cornish Coaster, 3.6%

Sharp's is best known for its bestselling Doom Bar, but it has a formidable range of other beers, of which Cornish Coaster is a memorable example. Dark gold in colour, there are hints of mint, citrus fruit and vanilla on the nose, while the palate has the soft billowing sweetness of malt, on which fruit notes make their mark. The finish is dry and bittersweet.

Date:

Your Rating: ☆ ☆ ☆ ☆ ☆

Skinner's
Betty Stogs, 4%

A quirky aspect of Skinner's public face is the use of characters from Cornish folklore for its beers' names. Cornish Knocker is one and then there is this lusciously fruity copper coloured bitter that is named after an ale loving, lazy good-for-nothing who reformed herself after the little people took her child away from her for a good wash in the morning dew.

Date:

Your Rating: ☆ ☆ ☆ ☆ ☆

Stonehenge
Danish Dynamite, 5%

Fruity golden ale from a brewery run by Dane Stig Andersen. On the nose there are bags of fruit and hops, with the tangy, pungent Cascade hop providing a lot of character. On the palate there's a grainy maltiness to start with, with a fruitiness emerging mid-palate before a big, slightly dry, bitter finish with fruitiness persisting. Very moreish.

Date:

Your Rating: ☆ ☆ ☆ ☆ ☆

Stroud
Budding, 4.5%

The inventor of the lawnmower Edwin Budding was the inspiration behind the name of this pale, refreshing beer, so it's entirely appropriate that it has a grassy, floral nose, thanks to late hopping with the aromatic Amarillo hop. This is very much a hop-driven beer with a luscious, citrusy palate and a bittersweet finish. One for supping after cutting the lawn.

Date:

Your Rating: ☆ ☆ ☆ ☆ ☆

Wadworth
Bishop's Tipple, 5%

If you want brewing tradition then Wadworth's has it by the drayload. Set in the middle of Devizes it is home to the famous 6X, but another favourite is Bishop's Tipple, formerly produced by the now-closed Gibbs Mew. Expect plenty of juicy, citrus tinged hoppiness on the palate and a measured bitterness.

Date:

Your Rating: ☆ ☆ ☆ ☆ ☆

TOP 10 BEERS

🍺 BEER	🍺 TASTING NOTES
Box Steam Funnel Blower	
Bristol Beer Factory Milk Stout	
Exmoor Beast	
Hop Back Summer Lightning	
Keystone Dark Porter	
Moor JJJ	
O'Hanlons Port Stout	
RCH East Street Cream	
St Austell Proper Job	
Wadworth Bishop's Tipple	

CENTRAL ENGLAND

The heart of England has beer running through its veins, whether it's the dark sweet traditional milds that sustained the working man of the West Midlands or the fruity and flinty pale ales that made the name of Burton-upon-Trent. Times change of course, and the love for golden ale is no less devotional here than in any other part of the country, but mild still holds its own in its heartland; further afield Hobsons (Shropshire) and Batemans (Lincolnshire) also brew particularly fine versions, while a fantastic version of a nineteenth-century strong mild is produced in Sedgeley by Sarah Hughes Brewery. Bitter is naturally big in the region, some more hoppy than others; Brewster's Hophead is a delightful well-hopped session beer. Innovation is not forgotten either as Derbyshire's eclectic brewery Thornbridge shows – their Jaipur is a ferociously fruity IPA delight. As for dark beers, Titantic Stout is a much-awarded classic, while new kids on the brewing block Blue Monkey keep winning friends with their Guerrilla Stout.

The Kean's Head, St Mary's Gate, Nottingham

Comfortable and airy one-room pub located in the middle of Nottingham's historic Lace Market. Owned by local pub company Tyne Mill, it has a superb selection of cask beers, including the absurdly delicious Castle Rock Harvest Ale. Good food, good beer and good vibes make this place a must.

Date:

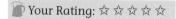 Your Rating: ☆ ☆ ☆ ☆ ☆

The Brunswick Inn, Railway Terrace, Derby

Atmospheric brewpub a few minutes' stroll from the station. Inside, it's a warren of rooms, including a cosy snug, while the main bar is overlooked and encircled by an imperious row of bottles on a ledge. Up to a dozen cask beers most days, including some brewed along the corridor. Triple Hop is particularly tasty.

Date:

 Your Rating: ☆ ☆ ☆ ☆ ☆

The Beacon Hotel, Bilston Street, Sedgley

Victorian hotel whose interior harks back to the days when pubs had separate rooms and beer was served to patrons at a hatch. An added bonus is the onsite tower-brewery that produces the marvellous Sarah Hughes Ruby Mild, a strong and rich mild based on a recipe devised by the current owner's grandmother.

Date:

 Your Rating: ☆ ☆ ☆ ☆ ☆

Barrels, St Owen Street, Hereford

Former coaching inn from the eighteenth century and a visual feast of wooden floors, exposed brickwork on which old enamel adverts hang plus a bar made from barrels. Originally the first home of Wye Valley Brewery, it is now the brewery's flagship pub where such delights as HPA and Dorothy Goodbody's beers can be found and enjoyed.

Date:

🍺 Your Rating: ☆ ☆ ☆ ☆ ☆

The Walter de Cantelupe, Main Road, Kempsey

Compact village inn named after a thirteenth-century bishop of nearby Worcester that provides a civilised watering hole for travellers on the nearby M5. Good food and beer are both pursued here with equal vigour, with the bittersweet and bracing King's Shilling from local brewers Cannon Royal being a particular favourite.

Date:

🍺 Your Rating: ☆ ☆ ☆ ☆ ☆

Batemans
Salem Porter, 4.7%

This is an award-winning dark beer from a much-loved Lincolnshire brewery. As dark as a moonless night this has chocolate and milky coffee on the nose accompanied by roast barley notes. The chocolate also comes through on the palate along with a rich, sweetish cold coffee-like character. The finish is dry and roasty.

Date:

Your Rating: ☆ ☆ ☆ ☆ ☆

Batemans
XXXB, 4.8%

Bitterness is very much to the fore on the nose and palate of this big-hearted and full-bodied copper-coloured beer. Fruitiness (restrained lemon notes) and a crisp cracker-like graininess on the nose, a complex bitter palate with more fruit, dry and crisp biscuity malt leads to the dry and intensely bitter finish.

Date:

Your Rating: ☆ ☆ ☆ ☆ ☆

Blue Monkey
Guerrilla Stout, 4.9%

This is a stately and elegant stout from a young East Midlands brewery that has already started winning them awards. The palate is creamy, smoky and brimming with espresso notes plus a hint of juicy plump currants usually found in a health shop's home-made muesli; there's toffee and caramel in the finish, along with some graininess.

Date:

Your Rating: ☆ ☆ ☆ ☆ ☆

Brewster's
Hophead, 3.6%

A 'brewster' was the old English term for a female brewer, so it's appropriate that Sara Barton is the founder of this Leicestershire brewery. Hophead is one of the brewery's bestsellers, a well-hopped session beer with plenty of citrusy fruit on the nose, while a sweetish, juicy maltiness and a delightful fruitiness leads to a bittersweet finish.

Date:

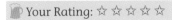 Your Rating: ☆ ☆ ☆ ☆ ☆

Burton Bridge
XL Mild, 4%

Classic mild from a micro-brewing pioneer in the former beer capital of England. In the glass the colour of bonfire toffee, its nose brings forth milk chocolate, milky coffee, roast grains and a hoppy earthiness (cf Burgundian earthiness). The palate is creamy, smoky, mocha, sooty, vinous almost, before its dry finish.

Date:

Your Rating: ☆ ☆ ☆ ☆ ☆

Castle Rock
Harvest Pale, 3.8%

Castle Rock brew their beers in Nottingham and their Harvest Pale is a light golden beer whose first impression is that it crackles with the scent of tropical fruit (think lychee and lime). The mouthfeel is equally fresh and fruity, crisp and satisfying leading to an appetisingly dry finish.

Date:

Your Rating: ☆ ☆ ☆ ☆ ☆

Everards
Old Original, 5.2%

Rich and sweetish, slightly roasted and port-like aromas announce the arrival of this venerable strong beer from Leicester's Everards. Reddish brown in the glass, it is rich and sumptuous, malty sweet, fruity and warming. Bitterness is restrained in the finish, with a return of the fruity and malty sweet notes.

Date:

Your Rating: ☆ ☆ ☆ ☆ ☆

Grainstore
Rutland Panther, 3.4%

Award-winning mild from Rutlandshire. The nose is coffee, chocolate and grainy – the latter reminiscent of a summer barn when it hasn't rained for a while. On the palate there is espresso, chocolate and a hint of fruity hop in the background. A beer to be enjoyed and contemplated on its own, or served with a Ploughman's.

Date:

Your Rating: ☆ ☆ ☆ ☆ ☆

Hobsons
Best Bitter, 3.8%

Shropshire is home territory for this thriving craft brewer whose mild is a recent Champion Beer of Britain. However, their Best Bitter is a tremendous beer as well, a classic session beer with a crisp biscuity malt character doing the tango alongside citrusy and fruity hop notes; the finish is bitter and slightly dry.

Date:

Your Rating: ☆ ☆ ☆ ☆ ☆

Malvern Hills
Black Pear, 4.4%

Standing at over 600 feet, Malvern Hills Brewery is reputed to be the highest in England. Since it began in 1998, it has won many awards for this gold-coloured session beer named after a locally grown pear. A light fruity and floral nose, while juicy, sweetish malt and chewy fruitiness lead to a long dry finish.

Date:

Your Rating: ☆ ☆ ☆ ☆ ☆

Marston's
Old Empire, 5.7%

IPA from Burton-on-Trent, which was where barrel upon barrel of this Victorian favourite trundled out to the Raj. Ironically enough, despite IPA's long history in the town, Old Empire is Marston's first stab at it. Deep orange hop notes on the nose, a soft malt presence on the palate, followed by a big bitterness that proceeds alongside a lingering dryness in the finish.

Date:

Your Rating: ☆ ☆ ☆ ☆ ☆

Nottingham
Extra Pale Ale, 3.8%

Pale sunlight in a glass, this award-winning ale from Nottingham Brewery has an array of delicate citrusy notes on the nose, veering towards lemon. In the glass it's a finely spun drop of succulently juicy maltiness working in tandem with smooth and soothing citrus fruitiness. The finish is dry and bittersweet.

Date:

Your Rating: ☆ ☆ ☆ ☆ ☆

Potbelly
Beijing Black, 4.4%

At 4.4% this mild is stronger than most, but it's a luscious drop promising a rich palate of toffee, grainy malt, milky coffee and dark fruit before wrapping it all up with a dry, sweetish roasty finish. The Kettering-based Potbelly only began brewing in 2005, and a year later Beijing Black was the Society of Independent Brewers' Supreme Champion.

Date:

Your Rating: ☆ ☆ ☆ ☆ ☆

Purity
Mad Goose, 4.2%

Purity plies its trade in the Warwickshire countryside. This light and sprightly blonde gets its name from the geese that wander about the brewery's perimeter. It's a very modern beer with a fresh and zesty citrus nose, a smooth, citrusy palate and an appetisingly dry finish.

Date:

Your Rating: ☆ ☆ ☆ ☆ ☆

Sarah Hughes
Ruby Mild, 6%

A mild at 6%, surely some mistake? But no, milds in the nineteenth century used to be much stronger than they are these days. Brewed at the back of the Beacon Hotel in Sedgeley to an original recipe, this is a gorgeously soothing beer that manages to have all manner of dark fruits on the palate along with coffee, chocolate and a dry slightly spicy finish.

Date:

Your Rating: ☆ ☆ ☆ ☆ ☆

Springhead
Roaring Meg, 5.5%

Big-hearted blonde ale from a brewery close to Newark-on-Trent. There's a gentle mingling of honey and soft fruitiness on the nose, plus orange marmalade. A burst of citrus flavour explodes within the mouth, there's rampant hoppiness with an undercurrent of grainy maltiness as the base. Dry, bitter finish.

Date:

Your Rating: ☆ ☆ ☆ ☆ ☆

Thornbridge
Jaipur, 5.9%

Innovative brewery based in the Derbyshire Peak District. This is their thoroughly modern take on the IPA, with a tremendous charge of citrus fruit on the nose (grapefruit, lychees even). The palate is soft, smooth and fruity, with a gentle honey-like sweetness in the background. The finish is long and bitter, demanding another sip.

Date:

Your Rating: ☆ ☆ ☆ ☆ ☆

Thornbridge
Saint Petersburg, 7.7%

Fantastic Imperial Russian Stout, dark and impenetrable in colour with an espresso coloured head. Complex nose: fiery alcohol, fruit gums, soot, mocha, condensed milk, cigar box; beguiling palate with more mocha and condensed milk, bitter fruit, hops and malty softness coming in, before leading to a long, lasting bitter finish.

Date:

Your Rating: ☆ ☆ ☆ ☆ ☆

HALF PINT

Titanic
Stout, 4.5%

Dark, dark brown in colour rather than midnight black, this is a classic full-bodied stout from the Potteries. The nose is a celebration of roast and toasted notes as a true stout should be; in the mouth it's full-bodied and rounded, creamy, also hints of treacle; it's also bittersweet and roast, before saying farewell with a lingering dryness and appetising bitterness.

Date:

Your Rating: ☆ ☆ ☆ ☆ ☆

Wye Valley
Dorothy Goodbody's Wholesome Stout, 4.6%

Dorothy Goodbody is a blonde bombshell who looks like she should be back in the 1950s with the likes of Diana Dors. She's not real, but a fictional pin-up who's given her name to several Wye Valley beers. This is one of them, a rich and roasted dark stout with plenty of coffee and chocolate flavours and a dry, lip-smackingly bitter finish.

Date:

Your Rating: ☆ ☆ ☆ ☆ ☆

Wye Valley
HPA, 4%

Herefordshire-based family brewery that celebrates its silver jubilee in 2010. This is its delectable pale ale (the H stands for Hereford, by the way), winsomely gold in colour, bursting with grapefruit and citrus fruit zest on the nose and more from the fruit bowl on the palate. The fruitiness is balanced by a light malt sweetness leading to a dry and bitter finish.

Date:

Your Rating: ☆ ☆ ☆ ☆ ☆

TOP 10 BEERS

🍺 BEER	🍺 TASTING NOTES
Batemans Salem Porter	
Blue Monkey Guerrilla Stout	
Castle Rock Harvest Pale	
Hobsons Best Bitter	
Malvern Hills Black Pear	
Marston's Old Empire	
Sarah Hughes Ruby Mild	
Thornbridge Jaipur	
Thornbridge Saint Petersburg	
Titanic Stout	

EASTERN ENGLAND

In the east of England many large and small brewers use locally grown barley, which is still malted in the region, though if you travel through towns such as Stowmarket the sight of converted malthouses tells its own story of the decline in the malting industry. Yet beer flows through this region, with many of the area's ales possessing a rich and deep malt character with an elegant balance of tangy fruity hoppiness. From its fastness at Bury St Edmunds, Greene King sends its beers throughout the country; some maybe feel aggrieved when they snap up a brewery, but there's no disputing their commitment to the cask-beer cause. By the seaside, Adnams still continue to enthral and enlighten many beer-lovers with their magnificent Bitter and Broadside, as well as other beers. Oakham go for gold with their beers and win gold as well, as do Crouch Vale in Essex; on the darker side of life, Bartrams offers up a soulful stout, while Mauldons' Black Adder is a delightful drop of darkness.

The Anchor, The Street, Walberswick, Suffolk

Prime example of the 1920s pub architectural style called Tudorbethan, the two-roomed bar is bright and comfortable, while a sea-facing terrace offers up space for al fresco eating and drinking. Landlord Mark Dorber is noted for his beer knowledge and at the bar plump for Adnams' stupendous beers, brewed in neighbouring Southwold.

Date:

Your Rating: ☆ ☆ ☆ ☆ ☆

Brewery Tap, Westgate, Peterborough

Until a couple of years ago this was the main home to Oakham Ales, whose brewing plant could be glimpsed behind glass. Now, the brewery has moved elsewhere, though the Tap still retains a brand-new brewing kit for experimental ales. This is a light and airy open space, modern and funky, and the ideal place to sample Oak's tremendous brews.

Date:

Your Rating: ☆ ☆ ☆ ☆ ☆

Cambridge Blue, Gwydir Street, Cambridge

This is an old-style two-roomed backstreet pub that boasts a modern feel, especially with the light and airy conservatory at the back. Located down a street of terraced houses, the interior is plain but comfortable (stripped wood floorboards) and over a dozen real ales add to the delightful atmosphere.

Date:

Your Rating: ☆ ☆ ☆ ☆ ☆

Thatchers Arms, Hall Road, Mount Bures, Essex

Refresh yourself with a pint of locally brewed Brewer's Gold from Crouch Vale at this welcoming rural inn on the Essex-Suffolk border. Sited in the middle of Constable Country, atop a ridge that overlooks both the Stour and Colne valleys, this is an ideal place to relax with a pint or two after a country ramble.

Date:

Your Rating: ☆ ☆ ☆ ☆ ☆

King's Head, Gorams Mill Lane, Laxfield, Suffolk

Thatched sixteenth-century village pub that is also called the Low House. Owned by Adnams, the interior is a warren of rooms dotted with ancient wooden settles while pictures of the village down the years on the wall tell their own story. Try the Adnams Bitter or Broadside which are dispensed straight from the cask.

Date:

Your Rating: ☆ ☆ ☆ ☆ ☆

Adnams
Best Bitter, 3.7%

Suffolk bitter from one of England's best-loved breweries. First brewed towards the end of 1960, this is a strong-armed beer with an earthy and scented orange hop character; this richness is counterpointed by a crisp biscuity maltiness. A dry and grainy finish invites the drinker to take another sip.

Date:

Your Rating: ☆ ☆ ☆ ☆ ☆

Adnams
Broadside, 4.7%

This beer first saw the light of day in 1972 in commemoration of the 300th anniversary of the Battle of Sole Bay. It was originally in bottle at 6.3%, but a more manageable draught version followed several years later. This is a tangy strong bitter that pulsates with citrus orange notes, well balanced by an urgent biscuity malt character.

Date:

Your Rating: ☆ ☆ ☆ ☆ ☆

Bartram's Comrade Bill Bartram's Egalitarian Anti Imperialist Soviet Stout, 6.9%

This small operation based just outside Bury St Edmunds has an excellent reputation. This is a dark, dark beer full of liquorice, chocolate, alcohol, mocha, currants and other dark stone fruits; the finish is a monster boost of dark roast malts and grainy dryness with a whisper of fruitiness.

Date:

Your Rating: ☆ ☆ ☆ ☆ ☆

B&T's Edwin Taylor's Extra Stout, 4.5%

Bedfordshire brewery B&T (formerly known as Banks and Taylor) has won several awards for this rich dark stout that bursts with nocturnal flavour, but is rather low in alcohol compared with many extra stouts and porters. Expect a roasty and sweetish nose and a complex palate in full-on seductive mode with creamy coffee notes and a dry bitter finish.

Date:

Your Rating: ☆ ☆ ☆ ☆ ☆

Crouch Vale Brewers Gold, 4%

Champion Beer of Britain in 2005, this Essex golden ale has passion fruit and a hint of grapefruit on the nose, with a subtle cereal background to remind you that this is a beer, not a juice. The fruit experience continues on the palate, kept in check with a fresh and spicy hoppiness and a touch of crisp grain, before descending into a lasting helter-skelter of a dry finish.

Date:

Your Rating: ☆ ☆ ☆ ☆ ☆

Elgood's Black Dog, 3.6%

Award-winning mild from a venerable Fenland family brewery. This is dark in colour with reddish tints, while on the nose there is a subtle resiny hop aroma (use pine resin as your guide) which is joined by the merest whisper of nuts (hazelnut?) The palate has roast and chocolate notes, before leading to a refreshing and slightly dry finish.

Date:

Your Rating: ☆ ☆ ☆ ☆ ☆

Greene King
Abbot, 5%

Godly ale from one of the biggest brewers of cask ale in the kingdom. On the nose a burst of caramel with a hint of citrus orange in the background; the palate is a rich act of worship at an altar containing nutty, malty sweet and citrus orange characters. The finish is dry and bitter. Look out for its winter older brother, the 6.5% Abbot Reserve.

Date:

🍺 Your Rating: ☆ ☆ ☆ ☆ ☆

Greene King Strong
Suffolk Vintage Ale, 6%

This is a blend of two beers, a 12% stock ale called Old 5X that is kept in wood for two years and a fresher and weaker bitter (BPA) that is a mere 5%. The two beers are married together and the result is this rich, vinous-tasting vintage ale that is an ideal companion when an aged Cheddar is brought to the table. Occasionally seen in cask.

Date:

🍺 Your Rating: ☆ ☆ ☆ ☆ ☆

Green Jack
Ripper, 8.5%

When this strong ale won Champion Winter Beer of the Year in 2007, CAMRA classified it as a barley wine, even though the brewery claims it as a Belgian-style ale. Blonde in colour, it has a deep fruity nose with hints of citrus in the background; on the palate the high alcohol gives it a warming effect with its malty sweet character balanced by a long bitter finish.

Date:

🍺 Your Rating: ☆ ☆ ☆ ☆ ☆

Mauldons
Black Adder, 5.3%

Another former Champion Beer of Britain, this bittersweet yet smoky stout comes from the Suffolk market town of Sudbury. Dark in colour, it has treacle, liquorice and roast malt on the nose, tempting the drinker further into its embrace with a rich, smoky, slightly sweet, coffee-like palate with hints of vanilla. A lasting, dry finish completes its impressive presence.

Date:

Your Rating: ☆ ☆ ☆ ☆ ☆

Mighty Oak
Maldon Gold, 3.7%

Essex brewery Mighty Oak celebrates its home base of Maldon with this luscious award-winner of a golden ale. As pale as sunlight, there's a delicate hint of citrus fruit on the nose (think tangerine) and the palate dips into the fruit-bowl for more citrus, while balancing it with breakfast cereal-like malt notes. A dry bittersweet finish encourages another sip.

Date:

Your Rating: ☆ ☆ ☆ ☆ ☆

Milton
Mammon, 7%

The village of Milton is just north of Cambridge, on the other side of the A45, and the ubiquitous brewery has made a name for itself with beers whose names and images celebrate Cambridge's erudite tradition. Mammon is a strong and rich dark ale, bittersweet and warming and just perfect for a winter's night, which is when it is available.

Date:

Your Rating: ☆ ☆ ☆ ☆ ☆

Nethergate
Old Growler, 5%

Suffolk porter that was named after a former head brewer's dog. Reddish brown in colour, there are hints of toffee and roast notes on the nose. The palate sings with toffee, chocolate and a pleasing hop character (think deep and ripe citrus skin) before rounding off with a long and complex finish that brings in a pleasing bitterness.

Date:

Your Rating: ☆ ☆ ☆ ☆ ☆

Oakham
Attila, 7.5%

Awards have always flown Oakham's way and in 2009 this belter was Champion Winter Beer of Britain. Classed as a barley wine, it has an aromatic nose of citrus and elderflower, while the fruit-bowl note continues on the palate with a full flush of ripe berries and more citrus with a warming alcohol note. The finish is long and bitter.

Date:

Your Rating: ☆ ☆ ☆ ☆ ☆

Oakham
JHB, 3.8%

Even though the brewery is named after Oakham, it's actually based in Peterborough and JHB is its mainstay beer, a fresh and fruity golden ale that was once Champion Beer of Britain. On the nose there's citrus and tropical fruit, while the palate sees a light, almost bubblegum fruitiness before a spicy, slightly bitter and citrusy finish.

Date:

Your Rating: ☆ ☆ ☆ ☆ ☆

Old Chimneys Brewery
Good King Henry, 9%

This imperial stout is named after a rare vegetable rather than anything royal and much married, and is dark as a moonless night. Fruit and roast notes on the nose, while the palate is soothing, warming, fruity and slightly sweet, finishing in a flourish of roasted barley and earthy hop. An 11% Special Reserve version is bottled.

Date:

🍺 Your Rating: ☆ ☆ ☆ ☆ ☆

St Peter's Fruit Beer
Grapefruit, 4.7%

Based in the Suffolk countryside close to Bungay, St Peter's has always been keen on producing a stunning variety of beers. Amongst its fruit beers, the grapefruit-flavoured one stands out. With the brewery's wheat beer as a base for the introduction of grapefruit flavouring, this is a zesty and refreshing fruity beer with a welcoming hop bitterness.

Date:

🍺 Your Rating: ☆ ☆ ☆ ☆ ☆

Wells
Bombardier, 4.3%

Even though 'The Drink of England' seems to have been around since before the introduction of the hop, it only appeared in 1980, but clever marketing allied with a well-crafted premium bitter has made it one of the leading cask ales. This is a beer with a spicy hop character and an underlying crispy biscuity maltiness that leads to a bittersweet finish.

Date:

🍺 Your Rating: ☆ ☆ ☆ ☆ ☆

Woodforde's Headcracker, 7%

Norfolk barley wine that is light as opposed to the usual chestnut-brown that one usually associates with the style. A daft name perhaps (encouraging inebriation rather than contemplation), but it's a peerless full-bodied drop with plenty of rich fruity character on the palate (plums and damsons). These are exquisitely balanced by citrus-like hop notes.

Date:

Your Rating: ☆ ☆ ☆ ☆ ☆

Woodforde's Wherry, 3.8%

In the past 25 years Woodforde's Wherry has established itself as one of the great bitters of England. Dark gold in colour (verging on a golden ale), it has a fresh, tangy citrusy nose courtesy of the Golding hop, with more citrus fruit (orange marmalade) and crisp biscuity graininess on the palate, leading to a lasting bitter finish with a growing dryness.

Date:

Your Rating: ☆ ☆ ☆ ☆ ☆

Young's Bitter, 3.7%

Formerly a London-based bitter brewed in Wandsworth, this classic session beer has survived its move to Bedford and the brewery's integration with Charles Wells (some might argue it has improved). It might not have its London provenance but it remains a sprightly, refreshing, lightly hopped beer that leaves a lasting dry, bittersweet finish at the end of the palate.

Date:

Your Rating: ☆ ☆ ☆ ☆ ☆

TOP 10 BEERS

🍺 BEER	🍺 TASTING NOTES
Adnams Best Bitter	
Bartram's Anti Imperialist Soviet Stout	
Crouch Vale Brewers Gold	
Elgood's Black Dog	
Greene King Abbot	
Green Jack Ripper	
Mauldons Black Adder	
Oakham JHB	
Woodforde's Headcracker	
Woodforde's Wherry	

NORTH-WEST ENGLAND

A region of contrasts: creamy amber ales and luscious dark milds, chestnut-coloured bitters and the odd ferociously strong barley wine vie for drinkers' attention in Lancashire and the surrounding north-west. Over in the Isle of Man, brewers have long had to contend with the Manx Beer Purity Law, which forbids anything but malt, hops, water, yeast and sugar in the making of beer; this doesn't seem to have done the island's largest brewer Okells any harm, though they needed the Manx parliament's approval for their wheat beer.

Manchester is a beating heart of brewing, boasting a healthy beer culture with a mixture of family brewers and small micros satisfying the Mancunian's legendary thirst; elsewhere in Lancashire Moorhouse's keep growing and also keep producing their distinctive beers. Further north in the Cumbrian Fells, micro-brewers mash and boil their beers with style and passion. What is it about beautiful surroundings that make people want to start a new life with a mash tun in tow?

Marble Arch, Rochdale Road, Manchester

Escape Mancunian bustle at this venerable pub with its own brewery. Inside, a reminder of Victorian glory: the words ALE, PORTER, RUM, WHISKIES, BRANDIES are picked out in a stone frieze running just below the ceiling. Time for a beer: take your pick from nine hand-pumps, five of which dispense Marble Brewery's excellent ale.

Date:

Your Rating: ☆ ☆ ☆ ☆ ☆

Doctor Duncan's, St John's Lane, Liverpool

Splendidly refurbished Victorian survivor in the city centre with lots of ceramic tile work and big open windows. It is owned by Cains Brewery so this is the place where you will get the very best of their beers including FA and Dark Mild; famously ran dry when Liverpool won the European Championship.

Date:

Your Rating: ☆ ☆ ☆ ☆ ☆

The Creek, Station Place, Peel, Isle of Man

Comfortable harbourside pub with dark wood fittings, traditional pub carpet, and nicotine-stained ceiling plus the feel of an old-fashioned station buffet, which it used to be. Situated opposite the House of Mannan Museum, it is an ideal place to spend time in the company of Okells' tangy, bittersweet Bitter.

Date:

Your Rating: ☆ ☆ ☆ ☆ ☆

Bhurtore Inn, Wrenbury Road, Aston, Cheshire

Well-regarded free house in the southern part of the county. Named after a city in northern India that a local landowner conquered in the nineteenth century, there are always eleven cask beers on tap, with many sourced from local brewers. The hearty food includes a selection of curries. Regular beer festivals held in July and November.

Date:

Your Rating: ☆ ☆ ☆ ☆ ☆

The Watermill Inn, Ings, Cumbria

Former lumber mill and guesthouse built from local stone and converted into a cosy and traditional-looking Lakeland pub in 1990 (Windermere is a couple of miles away). Up to sixteen cask beers are on offer (including the pub's own brewed selection). Eclectic interior including rocking chairs and a bar made with wood reclaimed from a church. Very dog-friendly.

Date:

Your Rating: ☆ ☆ ☆ ☆ ☆

Bank Top
Dark Mild, 4%

Bolton-based brewery whose traditional mild is a classic northern example of the style and complex with it. Dark in the glass it offers coffee beans, plain chocolate and hints of liquorice on the nose. The mouthfeel is smooth and creamy, with plenty going on as the roast and milky coffee notes testify, along with a suggestion of dark plum.

Date:

Your Rating: ☆ ☆ ☆ ☆ ☆

Cains
Dark Mild, 3.2%

Traditional northern mild the colour of Guinness, topped with a creamy, foamy collar. Complex palate has Dundee cake, Demarara sugar, evaporated milk, fruit, grainy maltiness and chocolate all vying for attention alongside a hint of resiny hop before the dry finish. The brewery is a spectacular Victorian-era red-brick terracotta palace in Toxteth, Liverpool.

Date:

Your Rating: ☆ ☆ ☆ ☆ ☆

Coniston
Bluebird Bitter, 3.6%

Named after the powerboat that Donald Campbell crashed to his death in on Coniston Water in 1967, this pale and winsome bitter has an abundance of spicy, bitter and citrusy notes on both the nose and palate, all balanced by a resolutely grainy malty base. The brewery is based at the back of the Black Bull Pub.

Date:

Your Rating: ☆ ☆ ☆ ☆ ☆

Dent
T'Owd Tup, 6%

Dent is in Cumbria but officially part of the Yorkshire Dales. Whatever the address, the fame of the village's eponymous brewery has travelled far, especially with the award-winning T'Owd Tup. Strong and hearty, this is a muscular, brawny stout where plenty of characteristic roast notes wrestle in the glass with a warming sweetness and dark fruit flavours.

Date:

Your Rating: ☆ ☆ ☆ ☆ ☆

Green Mill
Big Chief Bitter, 5.5%

The basement of an old woollen mill in Rochdale is the home of this relatively new brewery but they've already made their mark with this boldly hopped big hitter of a bitter, the elder brother of the brewery's weaker Chief. The use of American hops gives this beer a colourful range of aromas and flavour – including plenty of citrus and tropical fruit and hints of spice.

Date:

Your Rating: ☆ ☆ ☆ ☆ ☆

Hawkshead
Brodie's Prime, 4.9%

Since its arrival, Hawkshead has enjoyed considerable success, which has seen it move from its original home to nearby Staveley, where there is also an impressive brewery tap. Here devotees sample Brodie's Prime at the source, a dark voluptuous ale that delivers plenty of roast notes, working in tremendous tandem with a spicy fruity hop character.

Date:

Your Rating: ☆ ☆ ☆ ☆ ☆

Hesket Newmarket
Catbells Pale Ale, 5%

Cumbrian village pub and brewery that are owned by a local cooperative which helped save both operations from going under. Named after a popular fell in the Lake District, this is a light and refreshing pale ale with a tropical fruit nose, more fruit on the palate and a bittersweet finish.

Date:

Your Rating: ☆ ☆ ☆ ☆ ☆

Holt's
Mild, 3.2%

Mancunian brewers Joseph Holt are virtually unique in the British brewing industry in that such is the fast turnover of ale in some of their pubs that they are still supplied with 36-gallon hogsheads. The mild is one of the favourites, a traditional northern malt-edged version of its style, light to drink but with sweetish malt and roasty notes giving it bite.

Date:

Your Rating: ☆ ☆ ☆ ☆ ☆

Hyde's
Original Bitter, 3.8%

Classic Manchester bitter from a brewery that started off in the Victorian age and still remains in family hands. The nose is a mix and match of hop spice and malty sweetness, while the creamy and smooth palate offers a whisper of citrus fruit and crisp grainy cereal, before its long bitter finish.

Date:

Your Rating: ☆ ☆ ☆ ☆ ☆

Jennings
Snecklifter, 5.1%

Jennings is the largest and oldest brewery in Cumbria and this is its dark and strong winter warmer, which was first produced in 1990. On the nose a warming caramel-like sweetness with hints of dark fruits; the palate is rich, luxurious and touches base with chocolate and roast coffee bean notes, before its smooth dry finish.

Date:

Your Rating: ☆ ☆ ☆ ☆ ☆

Moorhouse's
Black Cat, 3.4%

Dark and smooth mild that was Champion Beer of Britain in 2000, offering a rare respite from the plethora of golden ale winners. Brewed in Burnley, this has a complex nose of milky coffee and chocolate as well as hints of an old-style tobacco box, while the palate is creamy, chocolaty and roasty and ends with a luscious dry finish.

Date:

Your Rating: ☆ ☆ ☆ ☆ ☆

Moorhouse's
Pride of Pendle, 4.1%

Moorhouse's brew their beers in the shadow of Pendle Hill, a place that naturally inspires the names of their beers (especially the notorious witch trials of the seventeenth century). This is their popular best bitter, pale amber in colour and a fruity little number (think grapefruit) with a long dry, grainy finish.

Date:

Your Rating: ☆ ☆ ☆ ☆ ☆

JW Lees
Bitter, 4%

Pale amber in colour, this is the bestseller of a family brewery that first fired up its brewing kettles just as Victoria was about to ascend the throne. As is common of beers of this style in the north-west, there's a fine balance between the sweetness of the malt and the hop-driven citrus fruit flavour. The finish is long and dry.

Date:

Your Rating: ☆ ☆ ☆ ☆ ☆

JW Lees
Moonraker, 7.5%

Dark brown barley wine from Manchester that gets its name from a local folk tale involving villagers, a rake, a pond, a large piece of cheese and the moon's reflection (make of that what you will). The creamy palate offers hints of treacle, mocha-ish coffee, chocolate plus an earthy hoppiness with a spiky hit of roastiness in the finish.

Date:

Your Rating: ☆ ☆ ☆ ☆ ☆

Marble Brewery
Stouter Stout, 4.7%

Home for this Manchester-based brewery is the Marble Arch, a survivor from the late Victorian/early Edwardian age of pub splendour. Stouter Stout, as the name suggests, is a dark beer with plenty of roast notes on the nose, while the palate offers a chewy and contemplative array of roast coffee and creamy notes, before its lip-smacking dry finish.

Date:

Your Rating: ☆ ☆ ☆ ☆ ☆

Okells
Aile, 4.8%

Okells brew in splendid isolation on the Isle of Man, but this doesn't mean that they are ignorant of what is going on in the wider beer world. Hence this luscious smoked porter, a real boon for those who like their dark beers to have some mystery. Smoky on the nose, it has a treacle and cream milky mocha coffee character on the palate; dry, smoky finish.

Date:

Your Rating: ☆ ☆ ☆ ☆ ☆

Okells
MacLir, 4.4%

Brewing on Man is governed by the Manx Beer Purity Law, which only allows beer to contain malt, hops, sugar, yeast and water. Okells' MacLir is a wheat beer, meaning that the brewery received special permission to brew it. It was worth the effort – this is a gently refreshing beer with a light lemony nose, and a luscious fruity palate, followed by a dry finish.

Date:

Your Rating: ☆ ☆ ☆ ☆ ☆

Phoenix
Wobbly Bob, 6%

Popular award-winning strong ale from a brewery that started life in Ellesmere Port before moving to Greater Manchester. Chestnut brown in colour, the nose offers a collection of sweet malt and nutty notes. The palate is full-bodied with caramel and a restrained sweetness working together with fruit before its big dry and tropical fruit finish.

Date:

Your Rating: ☆ ☆ ☆ ☆ ☆

Pictish
Alchemists' Ale, 4.3%

Alchemists' Ale is proof that brewers can turn malted barley, hops, water and yeast into pure award-winning beer gold. Pale in colour, there's a magical waft of hop-inspired tropical fruit on the nose, a theme that also occurs on the palate, interspersed with a crisp biscuity maltiness before its satisfyingly dry finish.

Date:

🍺 Your Rating: ☆ ☆ ☆ ☆ ☆

Robinson's
Old Tom, 8.5%

Classic winter warmer from Stockport that is superb in keeping out those cold Pennine winds. Almost black-blackcurrant in colour, it has a stupendous nose of toffee and malt followed by hints of caramel and fruit. A superbly balanced, mouth-filling, fruity, vinous and warming ale that also contains hints of the smokiness of whisky.

Date:

🍺 Your Rating: ☆ ☆ ☆ ☆ ☆

Weetwood
Oasthouse Gold, 5%

Weetwood was set up in 1993 at an equestrian centre just outside the large village of Tarporley in Cheshire. No prizes for guessing the colour of Oasthouse Gold, a beer that has won its fair share of awards. It's a fruity and smooth little number, deceptively drinkable for its strength and blessed with a dry citrusy finish.

Date:

🍺 Your Rating: ☆ ☆ ☆ ☆ ☆

TOP 10 BEERS

🍺 BEER	🍺 TASTING NOTES
Bank Top Dark Mild	
Dent T'Owd Tup	
Hawkshead Brodie's Prime	
Jennings Snecklifter	
Moorhouse's Black Cat	
Moorhouse's Pride of Pendle	
JW Lees Moonraker	
Okells Aile	
Phoenix Wobbly Bob	
Robinson's Old Tom	

NORTH-EAST ENGLAND

This is a large and robust area of beer patriotism. Yorkshire folk never tire of telling the rest of the world how good their beers are. Prepare to be enchanted by a stern bitter character working in concert with floral hop aromas; Timothy Taylor's Landlord is a case in point, while Acorn's Barnsley Bitter is an objective lesson in the attraction of bitterness. Harrowgate is home to Rooster's, where Sean Franklin works wonders with all manner of hops to fashion a series of gorgeous and elegant beers that win awards all over the world. Theakston's and Black Sheep continue to produce beers that make Masham great. Meanwhile, over towards Tyne and Wear, the appetite for brown ale continues even though the famous brand is now brewed in Yorkshire. Bittersweet cask ales with rich zingy hop aromas are now giving a choice to drinkers in the area. Look out for beers from the likes of Hadrian & Border, Jarrow and Wylam.

The Ship Inn, Low Newton by the Sea, Northumberland

Popular brew-pub in a small former fishing village, which is a picturesque National Trust-owned place complete with village green. A glass of Sandcastles at Dawn or Dolly Day Dream amidst the comfortably minimalist interior or outside overlooking the green and the sea beyond is the ideal pick-me-up after a ramble.

Date:

Your Rating: ☆ ☆ ☆ ☆ ☆

The Fleece Inn, Main Street, Haworth, West Yorkshire

Stone-built Victorian pub on the cobbled high street of a town famously associated with the Bröntes and, less famously, the film version of *The Railway Children*. The owner is Timothy Taylor, so this is a centre of beer excellence with all the brewery's beers on show alongside a selection of bottled European beers.

Date:

Your Rating: ☆ ☆ ☆ ☆ ☆

Kelham Island Tavern, Russell Street, Sheffield, South Yorkshire

CAMRA's Pub of the Year in 2008 and 2009, this is a traditional nineteenth-century local where northern friendliness comes alongside excellent beer, while the bar has the feel of a comfortable front parlour with cushioned chairs and heavy wood furniture. A dozen cask beers are on show including the full-bodied Barnsley Bitter.

Date:

Your Rating: ☆ ☆ ☆ ☆ ☆

The Cumberland Arms, Byker, Newcastle upon Tyne

Earthy two-roomed Victorian treasure that overlooks the old industrial centre of the Ouseburn Valley. It is also the unofficial home of traditional sword dancers the Newcastle Kingsmen. Beer rules, though not the brown ale that is now brewed in Yorkshire. Try Jarrow Bitter or the fresh and flowery Jetsam from Hadrian & Borders.

Date:

Your Rating: ☆ ☆ ☆ ☆ ☆

The Cross Keys, Water Lane, Leeds, West Yorkshire

Friendly and comfortable pub located in a post-industrial district not too far from the railway station. Interior is bare wood, massive beams and exposed brickwork, while the environment is friendly and comfortable – it's almost like a country pub in the city. Four cask ales – if it's on ask for Outlaw's creamy and aromatic Wild Mule.

Date:

Your Rating: ☆ ☆ ☆ ☆ ☆

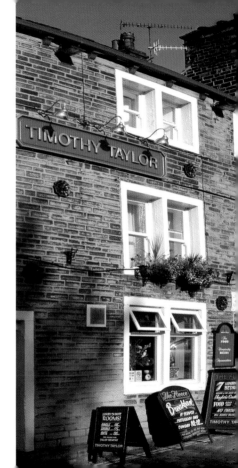

Abbeydale
Black Mass, 6.6%

Is it a stout or is it a porter? It's certainly as dark as the mass it's named after and at its strength you would feel devilish after too many. Whatever it is, Black Mass is an intensely flavoured beer, with leather saddle, treacle and roast coffee beans on the nose. The palate continues in a similarly exuberant vein with smoke, roast barley, dark fruits and a lingering bitter finish.

Date:

Your Rating: ☆ ☆ ☆ ☆ ☆

Acorn
Barnsley Bitter, 3.8%

The original Barnsley Bitter was a much-loved beer from a brewery that was closed when John Smith gobbled it up in the 1960s. Acorn's version (there is another Barnsley Bitter brewed by Oakwell) is a chestnut brown-coloured and full-bodied intensely bitter beer with roast/chocolate notes on both nose and palate and is immensely satisfying.

Date:

Your Rating: ☆ ☆ ☆ ☆ ☆

Black Sheep
Best Bitter, 3.8%

Black Sheep is famous for being set up by a member of the Theakston family after the family brewery was sold (hence the brewery name). This is their best-selling beer, a light golden bitter with a steadfastly hoppy character, offering torrid and tangy citrus fruit notes alongside a crisp graininess. Eminently drinkable.

Date:

Your Rating: ☆ ☆ ☆ ☆ ☆

Copper Dragon Golden Pippin, 3.9%

Lager lookalike from a Skipton-based brewery who moved into a new larger brewery in 2009. Light and refreshing nose offers gentle and delicate wisps of citrus (orange, grapefruit) plus an undercurrent of sweet grain; a juicy, citrusy mouthful of refreshment leads to a lingering dry bittersweet finish.

Date:

Your Rating: ☆ ☆ ☆ ☆ ☆

Crown Brewery Hillsborough Pale Ale, 3.9%

Small brewery based at the Hillsborough Hotel, which is part of Sheffield's famous 'real ale trail'. Pale blonde in colour, HPA has a zesty and forthright nose of bold citrus notes. This fruitiness continues on the palate (grapefruit and lemon), balanced by an appetising bitterness and followed by a long refreshing finish.

Date:

Your Rating: ☆ ☆ ☆ ☆ ☆

Double Maxim, 4.7%

When we think of a northeast brown ale we think of the famous one that keeps moving home, but Sunderland also had its own well-regarded brown ale, Double Maxim. Originally brewed by Vaux it was thought lost when the brewery closed, but has been resurrected. Expect a counterplay of spicy hop with a nutty, toffee-ish maltiness, before its bittersweet finish.

Date:

Your Rating: ☆ ☆ ☆ ☆ ☆

Durham
Evensong, 5%

In 1994 music teachers Steve and Christine Gibbs faced redundancy and were looking for something to do. They started Durham and haven't looked back since. Evensong is a ruby-coloured old ale/bitter hybrid with plenty of citrusy aromas and flavours, which are balanced by rich roasted, toasted and dark fruity notes.

Date:

🍺 Your Rating: ☆ ☆ ☆ ☆ ☆

Elland Brewery
1872 Porter, 6.5%

As dark as the darkest night, this creamy and full-bodied porter is currently Champion Winter Beer of Britain. Complexity is its middle name as one sip reveals a rich mouthfeel with hints of liquorice, light chocolate notes, some roast coffee beans and a mocha-like centre. The finish is bittersweet with roast notes.

Date:

🍺 Your Rating: ☆ ☆ ☆ ☆ ☆

Hadrian & Border
Farne Island Bitter, 4%

Amber-coloured best bitter with a crisp biscuity malty character that is mellowed out with smooth whispers of toffee and caramel plus a hint of soft fruit. In the finish a lingering bitterness takes a tango with a biscuity maltiness. Delicious beer that celebrates the Farne Islands, even though the brewery is based within Newcastle.

Date:

🍺 Your Rating: ☆ ☆ ☆ ☆ ☆

Hambleton Ales
Nightmare, 5%

Rich and dark stout from a Yorkshire brewery set up by former headmaster Nick Stafford. A former Champion Winter Beer of Britain, this is a smooth-drinking beer with a lightly roasted nose and an undercurrant of spicy hop; the palate melds in light roast, fruit and spicy hop notes to finish with a creamy slightly sweet finish.

Date:

Your Rating: ☆ ☆ ☆ ☆ ☆

Jarrow
Rivet Catcher, 4%

Yet another example of the thriving new wave of micro-brewing on the Tyneside in the past decade, Jarrow's award-winning Rivet Catcher is a gleaming golden ale with soft notes of fruit on the nose that continue onto the palate, working together with a crisp grainy maltiness to produce a light and refreshing beer.

Date:

Your Rating: ☆ ☆ ☆ ☆ ☆

Kelham Island
Pale Rider, 5.2%

Former Champion Beer of Britain and a mainstay of this popular Sheffield craft brewery based at the Fat Cat pub. It's a fragrant golden ale, replete with tropical fruit on the nose, a theme that continues onto the palate alongside a sherberty softness that is followed by a tingling bittersweet finish. Also try their Best Bitter.

Date:

Your Rating: ☆ ☆ ☆ ☆ ☆

Mordue
India Pale Ale, 5.1%

Mordue first hit the headlines when their Workie Ticket was Champion Beer of Britain in the late 1990s. This beer came afterwards, a modernist take on the IPA style that uses the American hop Horizon to deliver the aromatic and bittering intensity so necessary for an IPA. It works well and this beer bursts with citrus fruit, well-balanced bitterness and a crisp finish.

Date:

Your Rating: ☆ ☆ ☆ ☆ ☆

Ossett
Excelsior, 5.2%

Excelsior is the strongest regular beer from this West Yorkshire brewery. It's a dark golden strong ale with a fragrant fruity nose that draws the drinker in. Soft mouthfeel at first but then it becomes fuller with a tangy citrusy entrance plus some hints of vanilla. Finish is bitter and lingering with some crisp grainy malt making a brief reappearance.

Date:

Your Rating: ☆ ☆ ☆ ☆ ☆

Rooster's
Yankee, 4.3%

Yankee is an early example of the passion that Sean Franklin, the founder of this Yorkshire brewery, has for hops. American Cascade hops are used here to produce a stunning array of tropical fruit aromas (think lychee and even papaya), while the palate has a soft and caressing bitterness that is almost creamy. The sensuous fruitiness returns in the lingering finish.

Date:

Your Rating: ☆ ☆ ☆ ☆ ☆

Rudgate
Ruby Mild, 4.4%

This was Champion Beer of Britain in 2009 and being a mild it marked a change from the usual roll call of golden ale winners that has been the norm for the past few years. Brewed in Yorkshire, it is stronger than the usual milds and has more of a bitter character as well (raising eyebrows amongst the diehard mild drinkers). However, it's also smooth, smoky and luscious.

Date:

Your Rating: ☆ ☆ ☆ ☆ ☆

Saltaire
Triple Chocoholic, 4.8%

From Shipley with love comes this luscious and luxurious chocolate stout that uses chocolate malt, real chocolate and chocolate syrups. Yet despite all this chocolate it's not a sweet beer, being more like a hot chocolate with a creamy, soothing mouthfeel while a judicious hop bitterness keeps everything from toppling over into a tooth-jangling nightmare.

Date:

Your Rating: ☆ ☆ ☆ ☆ ☆

Timothy Taylor
Landlord, 4.3%

Several years back Madonna did no end of good for this traditional Yorkshire brewery by naming Landlord as her favourite tipple. And no wonder – it's a marvellous pale ale that sings with zestful and tangy citrus and floral notes on the nose, while the palate is a lively whirl of orange fruit, nutty maltiness and a long and loving bitterness.

Date:

Your Rating: ☆ ☆ ☆ ☆ ☆

Theakston
Old Peculier, 5.6%

Classic strong mahogany-coloured Yorkshire ale from the brewing town of Masham (Black Sheep is also based there). A smooth, warming and earthy nose with a background of sweetness (brown sugar?) leads to an all-enveloping, malt-led palate that conjures up dark fruit and rich toffee and caramel notes (but not too sweet) before its rich and mellow finish.

Date:

🍺 Your Rating: ☆ ☆ ☆ ☆ ☆

Wylam Brewery
Rocket, 5%

Heddon on the Wall in Northumbria is home for Wylam, in a collection of stone buildings very close to Hadrian's Wall. Rocket is an amber-coloured premium bitter with a flurry of delicate floral hop notes on the nose. The palate is refreshing and citrusy, while the finish is satisfyingly bittersweet.

Date:

🍺 Your Rating: ☆ ☆ ☆ ☆ ☆

York Centurion's Ghost
Ale, 5.4%

Situated within the city walls of York, so who's to know whether the beer's namesake might enjoy a drop on his ghostly perambulations? Chestnut brown in colour, the nose has plain chocolate and roasted coffee beans with a faint dusting of floral hop. The smooth palate has roasted malt, dark fruit and chocolate before its long bitter finish.

Date:

🍺 Your Rating: ☆ ☆ ☆ ☆ ☆

TOP 10 BEERS

🍺 BEER	🍺 TASTING NOTES
Abbeydale Black Mass	
Acorn Barnsley Bitter	
Black Sheep Best Bitter	
Hadrian & Border Farne Island Bitter	
Jarrow Rivet Catcher	
Rooster's Yankee	
Rudgate Ruby Mild	
Saltaire Triple Chocoholic	
Timothy Taylor Landlord	
York Centurion's Ghost Ale	

WALES

Bragget was the chosen drink of the ancient Welsh, a honey-based beverage; when the temperance bands ran rife in the nineteenth century, beer held firm. In the valleys, soothing milds and lightly hopped bitters made the Celtic soul sing, while further north beer tastes were more influenced by what went on over the border (Wrexham was also the centre of the eponymous lager brewery). Now, the Welsh brewing scene is diverse and full of energy and verve. Naturally, bittersweet golden ales are in the glass of many a

Welsh tippler, beers such as Snowdonia Ale and SA Gold, but some breweries such as Conwy add honey (an echo of bragget perhaps?), and others have been known to raid the kitchen garden for their beer – Otley makes a beer with rosemary. Brains is one of the great survivors. It's very hard to miss the brewery's name (both in Cardiff and further afield), whether emblazoned on the frontage of pubs and bars or on adverts extolling the virtues of the Welsh rugby team (which they sponsor).

PUBS

The Goat Major, High Street, Cardiff

Victorian city centre pub that attracts both locals and visitors and is ideal for a pre-rugby drop of Brains' splendid Dark. Inside, the interior dark wooden panelling and a tiled floor add to the traditional atmosphere, while the walls carry plenty of mementoes relating to the name — the Royal Welsh Regiment's tradition of a goat mascot.

Date:

Your Rating: ☆ ☆ ☆ ☆ ☆

The Bear Hotel, Brecon Road, Crickhowell, Powys

Historic coaching inn set right in the middle of this small town that lies between Brecon and Abergavenny. Rambling multi-roomed interior with plenty of wooden beams, comfortable armchairs and a sofa in the main bar add to the charms, while the cask beers include Brains' malty Reverend James. Excellent food.

Date:

Your Rating: ☆ ☆ ☆ ☆ ☆

The Crown, Pantygelli, Abergavenny

Three-storied coaching inn on the old Hereford road heading north out of Abergavenny boasting a history that reputedly dates back several centuries. The open-planned interior features exposed wooden beams, white-washed uneven stone walls and a cool slate floor. Great food (try the homemade scampi) and a selection of locally brewed ales make this a must.

Date:

Your Rating: ☆ ☆ ☆ ☆ ☆

Pen-y-Gwryd Hotel, Nant Gwynant, Gwynedd

Forbidding-looking but friendly establishment that has been a favourite of climbers since the nineteenth century. Located amidst the tremendous landscape of northern Snowdonia its style is simple and understated – wood and slate and the signatures of famous mountaineers. Food is locally sourced and the cask beer comes from Purple Moose in nearby Porthmadog.

Date:

Your Rating: ☆ ☆ ☆ ☆ ☆

The Penrhyn Arms, Pendre Road, Penrhynside, Llandudno

Community local that majors in cask beer and artisanal cider. Located in the hilltop village of Penrhynside, it's a bustling one-bar pub where locals and beer connoisseurs mix and mingle. Up to six cask beers are usually available. No food is regularly served, though pie and porter and cheese and beer nights are occasionally held.

Date:

Your Rating: ☆ ☆ ☆ ☆ ☆

Brains
Dark, 3.5%

Classic Cardiff mild that was originally called Red Dragon when first released; chocolate and coffee beans on the nose, then a full and well-rounded but refreshing palate that veers towards a modern porter with its creamy hints of condensed milk. There's a smooth finish with hints of fruit and a growing dryness.

Date:

Your Rating: ☆ ☆ ☆ ☆ ☆

Brains
SA Gold, 4.7%

Pale coloured and stronger sibling of the brewery's SA (famously known as 'skull attack'), and first launched in 2006. Fruit cocktail nose (citrus and summer fruits) with undertones of lightly toasted grains; palate engages with more citrus notes as well as a dry biscuity graininess while the finish is dry and bittersweet.

Date:

Your Rating: ☆ ☆ ☆ ☆ ☆

Breconshire
Golden Valley, 4.2%

Former Champion Beer of Wales and a consistent bestseller for the brewery. Amber-gold in colour, the nose offers a light and fresh floral aroma (is that a hint of mint?). In the mouth there's a soft billowing mouthfeel of malt breadiness working in tandem with deep citrus orange notes; the finish is bittersweet.

Date:

Your Rating: ☆ ☆ ☆ ☆ ☆

Breconshire
Ramblers' Ruin, 5%

An ale to sooth and suppli-cate after a day spent out in the immensity of the Brecon Beacons. It is dark amber in colour (the brewery call it an old ale), the nose has a delicious array of roast and caramel with an undertone of rich citrus; the palate continues in this warming theme before its dry and bitter finish.

Date:

Your Rating: ☆ ☆ ☆ ☆ ☆

Bryncelyn
Buddy Marvellous, 4%

Small brewery whose beers' names reflect the founder's love for Buddy Holly's music. This is an award-winning mild, ruby red in colour, whose roasted barley and chocolate nose is an immediate enticement. In the mouth the beer is an inviting blend of roast and chocolate notes with some sweetness; the finish continues dry and roasty.

Date:

Your Rating: ☆ ☆ ☆ ☆ ☆

Bryncelyn
Oh Boy, 4.5%

Yet another Bryncelyn beer with a Buddy Holly name; it is also another award-winner. This is a golden best bitter with an enticing bouquet of light citrus fruit, freshly cut grass and a light malty undertone. In the glass it's grassy and citrusy, crisp and fruity; the finish is long and lightly bitter.

Date:

Your Rating: ☆ ☆ ☆ ☆ ☆

Bullmastiff
Son of a Bitch, 6%

In the fast-moving world of Welsh craft brewing, Cardiff's Bullmastiff is a hardy survivor, having been at work since 1987. This is one of their best-known beers, a strong and warming amber-coloured creature that manages to bring together rich fruit flavours and serious malt notes, wrapping it all up in a striking bitter finish.

Date:

Your Rating: ☆ ☆ ☆ ☆ ☆

Celt Experience
Bronze Ale, 4.5%

Young Caerphilly-based craft brewery that celebrates all things Celtic. The brewery's beers are also organic. Bronze is a full-bodied, gold-coloured best bitter possessing a smooth mouthfeel along with delicate honey and fruit notes on the palate. Refreshingly dry bitter-sweet finish that also manages to find time for hints of toffee.

Date:

Your Rating: ☆ ☆ ☆ ☆ ☆

Conwy
Honey Fayre, 4.5%

Bestselling beer from a brewery situated on the edge of this famous castellated town. It's golden coloured and has a vibrant aromatic nose of floral frutiness and a hint of honeyed sweetness (local Snowdonia honey is used). It's full-bodied on the palate, fruity and sweetish, though not overtly honey-like. The finish has a pleasing bitter bite.

Date:

Your Rating: ☆ ☆ ☆ ☆ ☆

Conwy
Telford Porter, 5.5%

Dark chestnut in colour, this bittersweet porter offers gently roasted notes on the nose. In the mouth it is chocolatey and slightly sweetish with suggestions of liquorice and caramel adding to the complexity. All this is well balanced by a captivating bitterness. Named after the industrious Victorian bridge-builder Thomas Telford.

Date:

Your Rating: ☆ ☆ ☆ ☆ ☆

Cwmbran
Crow Valley Bitter, 4.2%

This is the bestselling beer of Cwmbran Brewery, a traditional copper-coloured best bitter that majors on a mixture of toasted malt and dark fruit such as raisins and currants. Malt sweetness dominates the palate at the start, joined by hints of roast barley and more fruitiness. The finish is dry and bittersweet.

Date:

Your Rating: ☆ ☆ ☆ ☆ ☆

Facer's
Landslide, 4.9%

Brewery that was started in the north-eastern county of Flintshire by a former head brewer at Boddingtons. This is fresh, fruity and fragrant on the nose, while there is a soft mouthfeel with hints of tangerine and honey on the palate. There's a dry grainy finish, which is joined by hints of nuttiness (hazelnut perhaps?).

Date:

Your Rating: ☆ ☆ ☆ ☆ ☆

Great Orme
Celtic Dragon, 4.5%

Golden ale with a luscious tropical fruit nose from this Conwy Valley brewery. The palate boasts a tremendously adroit balancing act between crisp biscuity malt and a surge of citrus fruitiness. The finish is dryish, before more fruit decides to come back into the equation alongside a bossy bitterness.

Date:

Your Rating: ☆ ☆ ☆ ☆ ☆

Great Orme
Welsh Black, 4%

The name might be a bit of a giveaway – yes this is a dark drop of ale, though despite its relatively low strength the brewery avoids categorising it as a mild. It's smooth in the mouth, luscious and luxurious, pulsating with chocolate and mocha coffee notes; there is a dry and grainy finish.

Date:

Your Rating: ☆ ☆ ☆ ☆ ☆

Kingstone
Classic, 4.5%

Microbrewery based on a smallholding in the Wye Valley near Tintern. Classic is a traditional full-bodied best bitter, amber in colour, and with floral and blackcurrant notes on the nose. Balance is key on the palate as malt sweetness and hop-derived fruitiness dovetail with each other. The finish is moderately dry with some sweetness.

Date:

Your Rating: ☆ ☆ ☆ ☆ ☆

Otley
O1, 4%

Modern forward-looking brewery based around Pontypridd. As the name suggests this was their debut beer when they launched in 2005. The colour of a sun-dried bale of summer hay, the nose thrums with floral and citrusy fruit notes. On the palate sensual citrus fruit and light caramel glide together, while the finish is thirst-quenchingly bitter and dry.

Date:

Your Rating: ☆ ☆ ☆ ☆ ☆

Otley
O8, 8%

Otley's well-placed sense of esteem served them well when they came to produce O8. At this strength expectations are high that the beer will be dark, but this is gold in the glass, with a rich, pungent fruity nose – citrus, ripe apricot skin. It's rich and indulgent in the mouth, dangerously easy to drink for its strength.

Date:

Your Rating: ☆ ☆ ☆ ☆ ☆

Purple Moose Dark Side of the Moose, 4.6%

Robust premium bitter that takes no prisoners. Chestnut coloured, it has roast barley and rich citrus on the nose. The palate is layered with more roast notes, coffee beans, some caramel all balanced by a rich citrus fruitiness. The finish is biscuity and dry. Known as Ochr Tywyll y Mŵs in Welsh.

Date:

Your Rating: ☆ ☆ ☆ ☆ ☆

Purple Moose
Snowdonia Ale, 3.6%

As Purple Moose brew on the edge of Snowdonia, then why not celebrate this splendid mountain range with a beer? Pale gold in colour, it has a fragrant and floral nose, while the palate is divinely balanced between a soft biscuity graininess and a juicy fruitiness. The finish is dry and bittersweet. Known as Cwrw Eryri in Welsh.

Rhymney
Dark, 4%

Rhymney are yet another example of the continuing renaissance of craft brewing in the South Wales valleys. The brewery is based in Dowlais and their Dark is a particular local favourite, being a generously malty mild/stout hybrid. It's creamy, smooth, caramelly and chocolaty, while the finish is dry and roasty.

Swansea
Three Cliffs Gold, 4.7%

Small brewery based at the Joiners Arms in the same Swansea suburb that Dylan Thomas came from. Pale gold in colour it has a light citrusy and floral nose, which leads to a fresh and fruity palate. The finish is dry and bitter and all the more attractive for it.

Date:

Your Rating: ☆ ☆ ☆ ☆ ☆

Date:

Your Rating: ☆ ☆ ☆ ☆ ☆

Date:

Your Rating: ☆ ☆ ☆ ☆ ☆

TOP 10 BEERS

 BEER    **TASTING NOTES**

Beer	Tasting Notes
Brains Dark	
Breconshire Ramblers Ruin	
Bryncelyn Buddy Marvellous	
Bullmastiff Son of a Bitch	
Conwy Telford Porter	
Facer's Landslide	
Great Orme Welsh Black	
Otley O8	
Purple Moose Snowdonia Ale	
Rhymney Dark	

SCOTLAND AND NORTHERN IRELAND

Even though whisky is Scotland's national drink, beer has always been there. Edinburgh was once called 'auld reekie', apparently because of the smell from its numerous breweries. Now, Caledonian remains the sole brewhouse in the city (and is owned by Heineken). Rich and dark Scotch Ales were once the chosen tipple of many a native drinker (though lager took an early stronghold in the country), often taken with a whisky chaser, but today's Scottish pubs are home to a new generation of sparklingly golden cask ales. Deuchars

IPA was the forerunner, but many craft brewers now offer sunlight in a glass. The old style beers have not been forgotten though, as Atlas' Three Sisters and Broughton's Old Jock demonstrate. Scotland is also home to innovation as Williams Brothers show with their beers made with heather and various other fruits and spices.

Over the water in Northern Ireland, Guinness still rules but the past few years have seen a small but growing group of craft brewers emerging, with Hilden and Whitewater to the fore.

The Bow Bar, West Bow, Edinburgh

Even though it looks like it's been around since Burke and Hare, this Old Town pub classic was only converted in the 1990s. Light and airy, its walls decorated with gleaming brewery mirrors, this is a high-ceilinged one-room bar with a good selection of cask beers served by the old Scottish Aitkens system of dispensation.

Date:

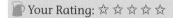 Your Rating: ☆ ☆ ☆ ☆ ☆

Old Inn, Gairloch, Wester Ross

This is a cosy and comfortable former coaching inn in the West Highland harbour town of Gairloch. It offers a wonderful selection of single malt whiskies as well as local cask beers, including locally brewed ones from the likes of the Dundonnell brewery and the leviathan-like strong ale Cullin Beast.

Date:

Your Rating: ☆ ☆ ☆ ☆ ☆

Blackfriars, Bell Street, Glasgow

Lively place located in the redeveloped Merchant City district of Glasgow, attracting a mixed bunch of customers (students come for the regular club nights in the basement). There's a long bar from where five cask beers are served, with the likes of Dark Star, Kelburn and Inveralmond being particular favourites. Good food is also served.

Date:

Your Rating: ☆ ☆ ☆ ☆ ☆

Moulin Inn, Kirkmichael Road, Moulin, Tayside

Friendly and busy edge-of-Highlands inn that has a history going back to the late seventeenth century. Charm and tradition aplenty inside: ancient wooden beams, stone fireplaces with roaring log fires and plenty of nooks and crannies. Meanwhile, an attached brewery produces a quartet of excellent cask beers.

Date:

🍺 Your Rating: ☆ ☆ ☆ ☆ ☆

The Crown Liquor Saloon, Great Victoria Street, Belfast

Unique pub that managed to weather the years and still looks like it has come out of Victorian Pub central casting. Snob screens, mosaic tiles, ornate mirrors, gas lighting and wood carvings are just some of the well-preserved features that make a visit to the Crown essential. Cask beers come from Hilden Brewery.

Date:

🍺 Your Rating: ☆ ☆ ☆ ☆ ☆

Arran
Blonde, 5%

Whether it's Arran, the Hebrides or Orkney, the Scottish islands are seemingly awash with craft breweries. This pale and aromatic beer has a flowery, gently citrus nose, while the palate is soothed and refreshed with a soft malty character that combines splendidly with a delicate citrus fruitiness.

Atlas
Three Sisters, 4.2%

Even though many modern Scottish ales veer towards blondness, Three Sisters is closer to the more traditional style of beer historically favoured by Scots drinkers: it's dark and rich with plenty of chocolate, coffee and malty aromas and flavours, while a juicy, tingling citrusy fruitiness offers a delightful counterpoint.

BrewDog
Punk IPA, 6%

This was the first release from a Scottish outfit that took the brewing scene by the scruff of the neck in 2007. Bitter on the palate, dry, full of tropical fruit (lychees, grapefruit, papaya), pungent, more American than an American IPA, peppery, spicy and more grapefruit. Immensely dry and spicy finish.

Date:

Your Rating: ☆ ☆ ☆ ☆ ☆

Date:

Your Rating: ☆ ☆ ☆ ☆ ☆

Date:

Your Rating: ☆ ☆ ☆ ☆ ☆

BrewDog
Rip Tide, 8%

Yet another example of how well BrewDog do when they take a classic beer style and give it a contemporary makeover. The style in question is Imperial Russian Stout and the result is a soothing and nourishing beer with a complex nose of chocolate, coffee and vanilla; the palate is rich, reviving, spiky and full of flavour. The finish is warming and invites the drinker to take another sip.

Date:

Your Rating: ☆ ☆ ☆ ☆ ☆

Broughton
Old Jock Ale, 6.7%

Excellent example of the old Scottish beer standard, the 'wee heavy', a strong and nutritious ale that was often drunk with a whisky chaser. Dark chestnut in colour, the nose is a powerful punch of dark roasted malt, warming alcohol and fruitcake; the palate is equally potent, matching rich malt sweetness, hop bitterness and hints of liquorice.

Date:

Your Rating: ☆ ☆ ☆ ☆ ☆

Cairngorm
Trade Winds, 4.3%

Light and spritzy, fragrant and floral, Trade Winds is at once a golden ale as well as an elderflower-infused speciality beer that almost drinks like a wheat beer. It has a clean and refreshing palate, upon which light fruity flavours dance, producing an appetising drink that well deserves its many awards.

Date:

Your Rating: ☆ ☆ ☆ ☆ ☆

Caledonian Deuchars IPA, 3.8%

Almost the colour of lager, this one-time Champion Beer of Britain has a fragrant fruit nose reminiscent of tropical fruit such as kiwi or pineapple, plus some soft maltiness (think gently toasted grain). On the palate, there's a great balance between a soft cereal-like maltiness and citrus fruit. The finish is dry and bittersweet.

Date:

Your Rating: ☆ ☆ ☆ ☆ ☆

Fyne Ales Piper's Gold, 3.8%

The northern end of Loch Fyne is home to the eponymous brewery. Piper's Gold is its handsome workhorse of a golden ale, a popular session beer that has also garnered several awards. Pale and ghostlike in the glass, this has delicate malt sweetness on the nose, while the palate is refreshing and becomes increasingly bitter with each sip.

Date:

Your Rating: ☆ ☆ ☆ ☆ ☆

Harviestoun Bitter & Twisted, 3.8%

Part of the new wave of Scottish blonde beers and a former Champion Beer of Britain. Gorgeous fruity aroma with hints of lychee, passion fruit, ripe melon skin and lemon. On the palate it's soft, malty at first, then there's tropical fruit in the middle, lemony, followed by a bitter and fruity finish.

Date:

Your Rating: ☆ ☆ ☆ ☆ ☆

Hebridean Berserker Export Pale Ale, 7.5%

Craft brewery based at Stornoway on the Isle of Lewis since 2001. This is their IPA, with the brewery claiming it is based on a 150-year-old recipe. Dark orange in colour, it has a rich and aromatic nose of both citrus and dark fruit, while the palate is warming, fruity (think raisins), earthy, malt sweetness before its spirited vinous finish.

Date:

Your Rating: ☆ ☆ ☆ ☆ ☆

Highland Orkney Blast, 6%

Small brewery situated at the northern end of the main Orkney island. This is a warming and strong-armed flaxen coloured ale that delivers a blast of rich fruit, hop-driven earthiness and biscuity malt on the nose; the palate veers towards the malt-store with grain and caramel, indulges in hop spiciness before its bittersweet spirituous finish.

Date:

Your Rating: ☆ ☆ ☆ ☆ ☆

Inveralmond Brewery Lia Fail, 4.7%

Crimson-chestnut in colour. There's a spicy punchy nose with a biscuity maltiness dancing in the background. Mocha coffee, chocolate and vanilla on the palate. Creamy, smooth, roasted coffee bean texture. This has an exquisite mouthful of flavour, and is well-balanced and malt-driven. Dry long finish with hints of stone fruit – raisin perhaps – and a roastiness.

Date:

Your Rating: ☆ ☆ ☆ ☆ ☆

Orkney
Dark Island, 4.6%

Dark chestnut in colour. The nose offers chocolate, coffee beans and hints of toffee. On the palate the initially grainy, bready notes are enlivened with chocolate, roast malt and a fruitiness at the back of the palate. The finish is lasting with roast notes and an appetising bitterness returning.

Date:

Your Rating: ☆ ☆ ☆ ☆ ☆

Orkney
Skullsplitter, 8.5%

'Wee heavy' that commemorates a long-dead Viking nobleman who was handy with the axe. Chestnut-red in colour, this has a powerful blast of fruitcake on the nose, backed by hints of ginger and vanilla. The mouthfeel is rich, heady, vinous and fruity, a complex palate of dried fruits, luxurious malt and rich spices. Dry spicy finish.

Date:

Your Rating: ☆ ☆ ☆ ☆ ☆

Traquair
Jacobite Ale, 8%

Aristocratic ale as dark as a mahogany sideboard, with a powerfully fragrant, spicy, almost perfumed nose offset by an undertow of sweet maltiness. It has a smooth and semi-creamy mouthfeel in which there is a refreshing herbal spiciness, liquorice, hints of milk chocolate and a citrusy marmalade character; its spicy, tangy finish lingers for a long while.

Date:

Your Rating: ☆ ☆ ☆ ☆ ☆

Williams Brothers Fraoch, 4.1%

Heather ale supposedly based on an old Gaelic recipe. It's an intriguing beer boasting a peaty floral nose, a dry malt character, spicy and herbal (think mint) notes on the palate and a dry and then vinous finish. Unique in that no hops are used – heather and sweet gale go into the boil instead.

Date:

Your Rating: ☆ ☆ ☆ ☆ ☆

Williams Brothers Midnight Sun, 5.6%

Midnight by name, midnight by colour, this is a very dark porter style given an extra edge by the use of fresh ginger in the brew. It's a complex drop, soft and silky in the mouth, as roast coffee beans, plain chocolate and hints of treacle run riot against this gentle background, along with a delicate ginger note.

Date:

Your Rating: ☆ ☆ ☆ ☆ ☆

Hilden Ale, 4%

Hilden was the first modern micro-brewery in Northern Ireland, setting itself up in 1981 amid the green and verdant countryside between Belfast and Lisburn. This is one of its earliest beers, a copper-coloured bitter bearing light aromas of citrus orange; in the mouth it's a pleasing combination of sweet maltiness and delicate fruit.

Date:

Your Rating: ☆ ☆ ☆ ☆ ☆

Hilden
Halt, 6.1%

Well-made example of the Irish red ale style, which has had a mild resurrection in the past couple of decades (though mainly in the US). Amber red in colour, this has nutty and gentle roast notes on the nose, is nutty, malty and fruity on the palate and finishes dry and bittersweet.

Date:

Your Rating: ☆ ☆ ☆ ☆ ☆

Whitewater
Belfast Ale, 4.5%

The Mountains of Mourne are home for Whitewater, who set up shop in 1996. This is their best-selling beer, an amber-coloured ale with a sweetish bready (even brioche) nose. Malt remains the master in the glass, sweetish and grainy, while there's also a creamy and luscious mouthfeel. The finish is smooth and dry.

Date:

Your Rating: ☆ ☆ ☆ ☆ ☆

Whitewater
Clotworthy Dobbin, 5%

The last Guinness porters vanished in the early part of the 1970s, but the reddish-chestnut Clotworthy Dobbin resurrects the style with great elegance. A complex and captivating cocktail of chocolate, mocha coffee and dark fruit works its wonder on the palate, aided by a citrus fruit punch courtesy of the inimitable Cascade hop.

Date:

Your Rating: ☆ ☆ ☆ ☆ ☆

TOP 10 BEERS

🍺 BEER	🍺 TASTING NOTES
Arran Blonde	
Atlas Three Sisters	
BrewDog IPA	
Broughton Old Jock	
Hebridean Berserker Export Pale Ale	
Inveralmond Brewery Lia Fail	
Orkney Skullsplitter	
Traquair Jacobite Ale	
Whitewater Belfast Ale	
Whitewater Clotworthy Dobbin	

FURTHER DRINKING

Brewery:

Beer:

Abv: %

Tasting Notes:

Date:

🍺 Your Rating: ☆ ☆ ☆ ☆ ☆

Brewery:

Beer:

Abv: %

Tasting Notes:

Date:

🍺 Your Rating: ☆ ☆ ☆ ☆ ☆

Brewery:

Beer:

Abv: %

Tasting Notes:

Date:

🍺 Your Rating: ☆ ☆ ☆ ☆ ☆

Brewery:

Beer:

Abv: %

Tasting Notes:

Date:

🍺 Your Rating: ☆ ☆ ☆ ☆ ☆

Brewery:

Beer:

Abv: %

Tasting Notes:

Date:

🍺 Your Rating: ☆ ☆ ☆ ☆ ☆

Brewery:

Beer:

Abv: %

Tasting Notes:

Date:

🍺 Your Rating: ☆ ☆ ☆ ☆ ☆

Brewery:

Beer:

Abv: %

Tasting Notes:

Date:

🍺 Your Rating: ☆ ☆ ☆ ☆ ☆

Brewery:

Beer:

Abv: %

Tasting Notes:

Date:

🍺 Your Rating: ☆ ☆ ☆ ☆ ☆

Brewery:

Beer:

Abv: %

Tasting Notes:

Date:

🍺 Your Rating: ☆ ☆ ☆ ☆ ☆